Praise for SQUASH THE SUNDAY SCARIES

"After years in the talent universe, I know firsthand that the hardest thing to rebuild in any organization isn't process or structure. It's trust, and in today's climate of burnout, layoffs, and constant change, it has never been more essential; Mary Baird gets that, and this book gives people leaders the practical roadmap to do the meaningful work of rebuilding it one experience at a time."

—**STEVE CADIGAN**, author of *Workquake*, Talent Strategist, LinkedIn's first CHRO

"This book cuts through the noise and focuses on what truly improves work: clarity, consistency, and leadership that people can rely on. Mary Baird, PHR makes employee experience simple and human, helping HR leaders create the conditions where people feel valued, supported, and able to show up as themselves." —**CLAUDE SILVER**, author of *Be Yourself at Work*, Chief Heart Officer, VaynerX

"With *Squash the Sunday Scaries*, Mary provides a volume with hundreds of practical action-steps and numerous real-life examples for leaders. If you walk away from this book not knowing practical steps to take to significantly improve your workplace culture, you have only yourself to blame! This is a wonderful resource for leaders at any level."

—**DR. PAUL WHITE**, co-author of *The 5 Languages of Appreciation in the Workplace*, President, Appreciation at Work

"*Squash the Sunday Scaries* gives HR leaders practical tools they can use immediately to create positive change at work. It's clear, grounded, and designed for real-world application, not theory. This book offers a blueprint for repairing the fractured social contract between employers and employees by intentionally redesigning the employee experience. With a clear focus on trust, fairness, and meaningful work, it provides leaders with concrete steps they can implement immediately to create lasting organizational impact."

—**ERIN SWAIN**, Director of Learning and Development, DallasHR

"If you're trying to repair a broken culture and ignite performance, you need more than good intentions—you need a plan. Mary's flywheel approach is clear, practical, and immediately usable. It helps you focus on what drives employee experience, take action quickly, and be the hero to your executive team."
—**DR. ALISE CORTEZ**, author of *The Great Revitalization* and *Purpose Ignited*, Chief Ignition Officer, Gusto, Now!

"Culture doesn't change because of programs—it changes when leaders are aligned. How leaders show up, how teams work together, and how employees experience the organization all flow from our values. This book shows leaders how to translate values into everyday leadership practices, turning employee experience into a meaningful and measurable business advantage."
—**HOLLY NOVAK, SPHR, SHRM-SCP**, Chief People Officer, Jack Henry & Associates

"Mary has written a practical and deeply human playbook that replaces surface-level perks with a scalable system to rebuild trust, transform culture, and turn Sunday dread into Monday momentum. If you deal with people, you need to read this book." —**DR. TONY BRIDWELL**, author of *Beyond the Leader: A Fable About the 7 Disciplines that Define Extraordinary Teams*, Chief Talent Officer, The Encompass Group

"Mary Baird shows what often gets lost in organizations: succession planning isn't just names on a spreadsheet, it's an active system that fuels continuity and growth. *Squash the Sunday Scaries* offers HR and people leaders practical, usable tools to build leadership bench strength, accelerate internal mobility, and reduce risk well before it becomes urgent." —**THERESA CARIK, Ph.D.**, Principal Consulting Psychologist, Chapman & Co. Leadership Institute

"*Squash the Sunday Scaries* highlights a critical viewpoint—shifting the conversation about burnout from an individual resilience problem to an issue of organizational responsibility. By focusing on improving the employee experience, this playbook offers practical guidance for HR, culture, and people leaders who want to redesign work in ways that don't quietly erode people's well-being or demand self-sacrifice for success."
—**MEGHAN FRENCH DUNBAR**, author of *This Isn't Working*, Entrepreneur

Praise for THE SIMPLIFIERS PODCAST

"Mary Baird is the real deal. She's curious, warm, and wicked smart. The Simplifiers Podcast delivers big insights in the most human way possible. It feels like sitting down with your smartest friend for coffee and leaving inspired." —**KRISTIN BOCK,** TEDx Speaker, Body Language & Communication Consultant, Body Language Blueprints

"Not only is Mary an incredible host—she's brilliant, smart, and brings her own experience to the conversation which benefits everyone. Many thanks for the opportunity to contribute to your passion of making life simple and BETTER!" —**LEFTYRASTA,** review on Apple Podcasts from a listener

"I've done many interviews, and Mary Baird is a superb and professional interviewer. Prior to the interview, she sends reminders, asks for sufficient information to enable her to prepare, leading to a meaningful conversation. It's clear that she's done her homework. Some people have high standards and raise the bar — Mary is one of the best!" —**DAN MILLMAN,** author of *Way of the Peaceful Warrior* and *Peaceful Heart, Warrior Spirit*

"Mary is an excellent interviewer. She is thorough, yet entertaining to keep your attention during the entire episode. I really enjoy the guests she has on the show on their own, but with the questions she asks, she takes their expertise to the next level." —**LEH820,** review on Apple Podcasts from a listener

"This podcast is for busy people in need of simple-yet-powerful advice. Mary is awesome at exploring often uncomfortable topics with grace and offering advice that's easy to implement." —**JOVANKA CIARES,** author of *Reclaiming Wellness,* Integrative Herbalist, Nutrition Coach

"I needed this podcast in my life today. Mary's calm voice really makes listening feel more like a meditation." —**MARATHON DOGMOM,** review on Apple Podcasts from a listener

"Mary is such a wonderful interviewer! Her podcast feels like you get to listen in on a conversation with really smart folks who are relatable and conversational."
—**LIBBY MAGLIOLO,** Founder & CEO, The Slide Master

"Who doesn't want life simplified? If your life, or parts of it, seem complicated, this podcast is for you. Mary does a great job covering all aspects of life and simplifying them. She is a great interviewer and has great insight on life. The tips on this show are not only great life hacks, but will provide you how to live with more ease daily."
—**LIVINGALIVE123!,** review on Apple Podcasts from a listener

"I'm touched by the work that you do, so thank you for having genuine conversations. It's meaningful. Thank you for simplifying how to be a good human."
—**JUSTIN JONES-FOSU,** author of *I Respectfully Disagree* and *The Inclusive Mindset,* Keynote Speaker

Mary interviewing Dr. Gary Chapman, author of the 5 Love Languages, on The Simplifiers Podcast

Listen to The Simplifiers Podcast wherever you get your podcasts, including Apple Podcasts and Spotify, and visit www.thesimplifiers.com for the show notes.

SQUASH the SUNDAY SCARIES

A Modern Playbook to Rebuild Trust, Transform Culture, and Reignite Your Workforce

Publisher: The Simplifiers Press

Cover Design by The Simplifiers

Interior Design by Zoe Norvell

ISBNs:

979-8-218-93832-1 (paperback)

979-8-9954927-3-3 (ebook)

979-8-9954927-9-5 (audiobook)

Library of Congress Control Number: 2026908169

Disclaimer

The author is not an attorney or licensed professional, and this book is not intended to provide legal, regulatory, or compliance advice. The content is shared for educational and informational purposes only, based on the author's experience working in human resources, leadership development, employee experience, and organizational culture.

Workplace laws, regulations, company policies, and employment practices vary by organization, industry, and jurisdiction and are subject to change. While every effort has been made to ensure the accuracy of the information at the time of publication, this book does not offer an exhaustive treatment of any topic and should not be relied upon as a substitute for professional, legal, or HR advice specific to your situation.

The author and publisher assume no responsibility for errors, omissions, or outcomes resulting from the use or application of the information in this book. You are solely responsible for your decisions, actions, and results. Readers are encouraged to consult qualified legal counsel and/or business professionals before implementing policies, practices, or organizational changes.

First Edition

Visit the author online at:
www.marybaird.co | www.thesimplifiers.com

SQUASH THE SUNDAY SCARIES

A Modern Playbook to Rebuild Trust, Transform Culture, and Reignite Your Workforce

The Simplifiers Guide
to Better Employee Experience

Mary Baird, PHR

The Simplifiers Press

Frisco, Texas, USA

Calling All Simplifiers!

Congrats! By owning this book, you've joined a global community of Simplifiers. People who want to make work better and help others squash the Sunday Scaries, too.

This book was written to help you take simple, practical action.

Not just for yourself, but for your team, your workplace, and the people you lead.

Here's how to keep the momentum going:

Spread the word

If this book helped you, please leave a review on Amazon, Goodreads, or wherever you buy books. Your review helps more HR leaders, managers, and teams discover these ideas and do the thing.

Bring this work to your team

Bring Mary in to speak at your next conference, HR team meeting, ERG event, affinity group, strategic retreat, off-site, or leadership program. You can also book an interactive workshop, in person or virtual, for your HR team or people managers who want practical ways to put this work into practice.

Get plugged in with The Simplifiers

Listen to and subscribe to The Simplifiers Podcast on Apple Podcasts, Spotify, or your favorite podcast app for weekly conversations that simplify work, life, and everything in between. Also, sign up for The Simplifiers Super Insiders email newsletter for practical ideas, tools, and updates at www.thesimplifiers.com

Take the next step

Want hands-on support? Book The Simplifiers 30-Day EX Accelerator to launch your first employee listening pulse, uncover your biggest areas of opportunity, and build a focused 90-day action plan with Mary and her team's guidance.

Need bulk book orders for your HR team, next event, or book club?

Contact hello@marybaird.co for details.

Have a question?

Connect with Mary on LinkedIn, mention you read the book, and send her a DM: www.linkedin.com/in/thesimplifiers

To learn more about speaking, workshops, the EX Accelerator, and consulting, visit www.marybaird.co.

Let's simplify work, together.

TABLE OF CONTENTS

The Simplifiers Employee Experience Flywheel™

To Zoë and Otto:
I love you both so much and
I hope you think this is cool.

To 8-year old Mary:
You simply being you
makes a positive impact on the world.
Never forget that.

FOREWORD

FOREWORD

By Jimmy Taylor, SPHR - Executive Director, DallasHR

There has never been a time in my career when human resources has felt this overwhelmed, and I don't say that lightly.

From my vantage point as Executive Director of DallasHR, I work with HR leaders across multiple industries and organizations. What feels heavier today, even more than five years ago, is not just the work itself but the pace of it. The speed of change has accelerated, expectations have multiplied, and HR leaders are being asked to do more with fewer resources at precisely the moment when the stakes feel higher than ever.

Technology, especially AI, has amplified this reality.

Most HR professionals know they should be doing something with it, but many don't know where to start. They're trying to keep up, learn new tools, support leaders, stay compliant, steady their employees, and still somehow "fix the culture," often all at once.

It's exhausting.

What I hear most often is not a lack of commitment or care. It's real fatigue. HR leaders are waking up every morning already behind, navigating what feels like a never-ending string of challenges, and trying to hold things together while standing in the middle of the storm. And yet, despite all of that pressure, they still feel deeply responsible for making work better for their people and for the organization as a whole.

That's why this book matters right now.

Employee experience is often discussed in abstract terms, but in practice, it's much simpler and much more personal. It's the emotional impact work has on people. Our workplaces change us. The real question is whether they change us in healthy, positive ways or in ways that leave people depleted, disconnected, and disengaged. Over time, those experiences shape how people show up, not just at work but in their lives.

From everything I've seen, no single factor influences that experience more than the first-level people manager. Culture programs, benefits, and perks matter, but they will never outweigh the daily reality of who someone reports to. That relationship, especially in the first 90 days, is incredibly powerful. It's when attachment is formed, trust is built, and expectations are set. If that attachment is broken, the only real way to change it is to change the manager or change how that manager leads.

And yet, organizations continue to overcomplicate employee experience by focusing on big, expensive initiatives while overlooking the small, human moments that matter most. Simple conversations. Clear expectations. Feeling heard. Understanding how one's work connects to the larger purpose of the organization. These are not glamorous fixes, but they are the ones that move the needle.

I've seen this work in real life. At a Canadian manufacturing company, leaders encouraged employees at every level to spend just fifteen minutes a few times a week working on something that bothered them in their day-to-day work. No big budget. No complex program. That simple act of listening and ownership led to meaningful improvements in quality, productivity, and engagement because employees could see how their ideas directly shaped the work. It was a powerful reminder that culture doesn't change through grand gestures, but through consistent, human ones.

This is where HR's role has expanded, and where it has also become more challenging. HR cannot fix culture alone. Shaping employee experience is everyone's responsibility, especially the leadership team's. But HR is uniquely positioned to equip managers, model the right behaviors, and bring clarity where there is confusion, even when outcomes are not fully within HR's control.

The most effective HR leaders I see today aren't waiting for perfect conditions. They're listening carefully, prioritizing what's actually broken, and starting where they are. They use AI where it makes sense. They bring managers practical tools, not theory. And when they get small wins, they use those results to build credibility and momentum.

That's why *Squash the Sunday Scaries* is so timely and so needed.

Mary Baird understands this reality deeply. She's not writing from the sidelines or from a purely academic perspective. She's spent years doing the work, teaching, listening, testing, and refining what actually helps HR leaders make progress when things feel messy and overwhelming.

Mary is the voice of modern HR—she simplifies it in a fresh way so you can take action and get results, fast!

This book doesn't ask you to fix everything at once. It gives you permission to start with Employee Listening, then focus on one chapter, one lever, and one practical action you can take right now.

This book bridges the gap between feeling overwhelmed and knowing where to begin. It meets HR leaders like you where you are and offers practical ideas for making immediate, meaningful impact without adding more complexity to an already full plate. I love that Mary's company is called The Simplifiers because that's exactly what she does. She makes it simple to understand and gives you the insider's playbook to take action.

If you're feeling overwhelmed, know this: you've already lived through one of the most tumultuous periods in the history of modern HR, from 2020 to the present. And while the next five to ten years may bring even more change, you don't have to navigate it without clarity or direction.

Start here. Use what you need. And take the next right step.

WHY WORK
FEELS
BROKEN

INTRODUCTION

Why Work Feels Broken

*"People are asked to give their best inside systems
that bring out their worst."*

—Mary

Every Sunday night, millions of workers feel it—the piercing thrum of total dread as the weekend fades away.

What do you do? Pop an ibuprofen. Binge another show. Question your life choices and scream into the void. You know, the usual.

All the while, the unread emails are piling up. The broken processes await. And that 8 a.m. Monday morning readout call is sitting on your calendar, mocking you from afar. Plus, if you work in HR, well, this hits twice as hard because you not only shoulder your own worries, but everyone else's too. I mean, you're the People people. *This is your job, right?*

Spoiler alert: this isn't just fatigue. It's something deeper. First came "quiet quitting": disengage, do the bare minimum, get through the day. Then came "quiet cracking": smart, committed people still show up and still hit deadlines, but with clenched jaws and hollow eyes, one more fire drill away from burnout or an unexpected leave of absence.

And now, I call it "simply surviving," when work becomes endurance: minimal extra effort, low connection, and someone who disappears a little more each week.

Employees aren't choosing to coast, they're barely holding on.

The old model—*show up, get paid, stay loyal*—no longer holds, especially after waves of layoffs, shifting goals, and the dizzying whiplash of AI, automation, and technological change.

Employees want transparency, not spin; purpose, not platitudes; and leadership that keeps its promises. All the while, organizations still need profit, innovation, and performance from their workforce. Somewhere in the middle, trust cracked on both sides.

And here's the business risk hiding in plain sight: when managers disengage, teams usually follow. Gallup's 2025 *State of the Global Workplace* report found that only 27% of managers globally are engaged at work, and Gallup's broader research shows that managers account for 70% of the variance in team engagement. In other words, disengagement at the manager level ripples outward fast. People may still be showing up, but too often they're clocking in, clocking out, doing the bare minimum, and delivering solid C- work.

Disengaged managers

create

disengaged teams.

That's why the paradigm at the heart of this book matters so much:

Better Employee Experience (EX) =

Better Customer Experience (CX) =

Better Business Results.

Across the board, the signal is clear: burnout prevention, retention, and trust-building are the top HR agenda items in the year ahead. And 88% of HR professionals say HR must play a more active role in shaping business strategy, not just managing operations.

So let's be real: if you're reading this, you feel the divide, too.

You've seen the ripple effects: burned-out teams, elusive accountability, leaders who care but lack a shared playbook, and wary customers who sense the wobble. You've tried perks like pizza parties and ping-pong tables. You've launched surveys where nothing happens. You've rolled out toolkits with little to no adoption.

And still, that sick-to-your-stomach Sunday night ulcer feeling remains.

This book is about repairing that crack in the foundation—simply, practically, and humanely—by redesigning the *employee experience* people actually have at work. Not with slogans. Not with company-branded swag. *(I mean, c'mon… who needs another water bottle?!)* But rather, with a repeatable system your workforce actually appreciates, and one you can put in motion next Monday to scale across the enterprise.

The crack in the social contract (what broke & why now)

The traditional contract of work, as in "stability in exchange for loyalty," frayed long before the pandemic, but the last few years accelerated the tear. The ground shifted fast: hybrid work created new expectations for flexibility and fairness. AI promised efficiency, yet stirred uncertainty. Cost pressures drove knee-jerk restructuring and layoffs. Trust was tested by half-answers and hurried change. Amid the noise, a new contract is emerging, one rooted in transparency, fairness, and meaningful work.

Employees are asking straightforward questions:

- *Where are we going, and why does it matter?*
- *What's expected of me this quarter, specifically?*
- *Will you tell me the truth, even when it's hard?*
- *Will you invest in my growth?*
- *Will you advocate for me (and my role) in rooms where I'm not present?*
- *Do my daily tools and rituals help me do my best work, or get in the way?*

Organizations are asking equally pragmatic ones:

- *How do we perform consistently in a volatile market?*
- *How do we innovate without burning people out?*
- *How do we get lean and profitable without sacrificing our world-class customer experience?*
- *How do we keep our promises—to customers, investors, and employees—all at the same time?*
- *Do these people actually want to work… or not?!*

These are not competing questions.
They are two sides of one coin.

The bridge is Employee Experience, otherwise known as "EX": the sum of what people live every day while they are at work, from the first touchpoint to the last, across tools, spaces, roles, and relationships.

When EX is designed with intention, trust strengthens, performance rises, and ultimately, your customers feel the difference.

The Simplifiers Employee Experience Flywheel™

You see, great EX isn't a one-off initiative. It's a flywheel, a small set of reinforcing moves that create momentum when you keep your hand on them.

The first step is always the same:

Employee Listening with the Intent to Act → Gather data from your employees on what's broken, where there's opportunity, and prioritize where to go on the flywheel next to fix things and improve the employee experience.

And that's the beauty of the flywheel: it's meant to be <u>cyclical</u>, not sequential. So once you've gathered the clues from your workforce, spin the wheel, and simplify down to the one area you need to focus on next, such as:

- Employer Branding That Matches the Inside
- Talent Assessments That See the Whole Human
- Leadership Development for a Skills-Based Workforce
- Succession Planning: Make a Plan for Now vs. Next
- Recognition + Engagement: From Performative to Powerful
- New Hire Onboarding That Feels Like Belonging
- The Digital Employee Experience (That Isn't From 1986)
- Workplace Experience: Rethinking the Office Space for Modern Hybrid Success
- The People Leader's Playbook: Integrity in Action
- Better EX = Better CX = Better Business Results: Culture as a Competitive Advantage
- Your Action Plan for Next Monday

Sound like a lot? Just remember, you don't have to master all of it at once. Start the flywheel with Employee Listening, determine your EX roadmap, keep your hands on the wheel, and let the momentum compound.

It's a choose-your-own-adventure book!

And here's the best part: just like your favorite choose-your-own-adventure books from childhood, turn to the chapter you need most, when you need it. In fact, this playbook isn't meant to be read in sequential order. Use it where you need it, right in the moment.

I also really encourage you to write in the margins, scribble notes, earmark your favorite pages, and make it your own. This is your playbook, your reference guide, and your compass for the year ahead. So get messy with it. Underline what matters. Circle what hits. Jot down the ideas you want to try next. It's yours.

My hope is that a year from now, this book has a well-worn spine because it's your trusty, go-to guide that you reference every single week.

Start in the middle of the flywheel and then choose-your-own-adventure and decide where you want to go next!

The Simplifiers Employee Experience Flywheel™

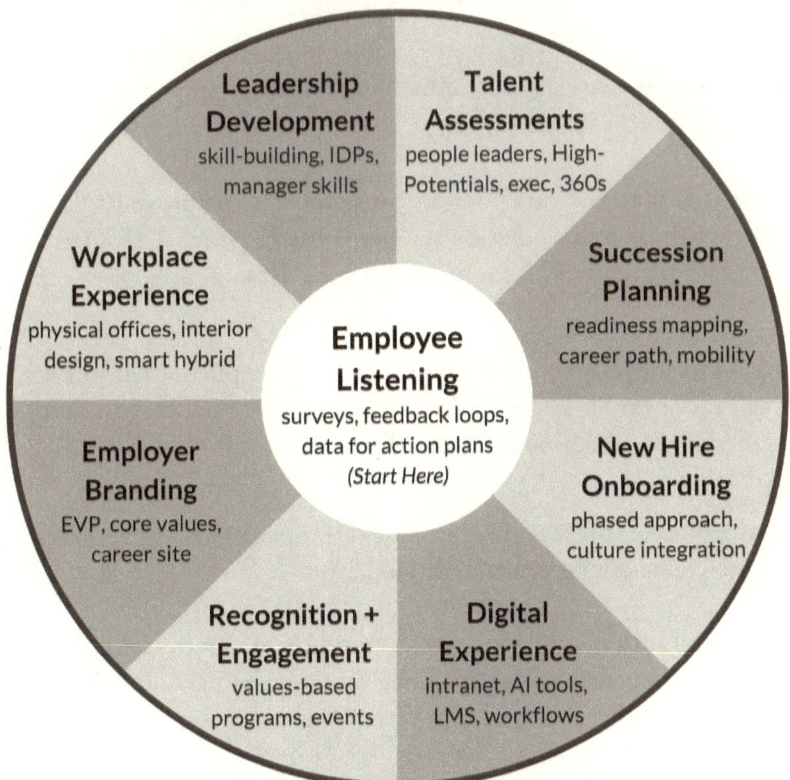

How this book works

We are The Simplifiers, so that means we promise to keep things simple! Therefore, every chapter follows a repeatable, simplified format:

What it is, simplified. – a clear, simplified definition.

Why it matters now – urgency, context, and data that makes the case.

Common mistakes & pitfalls – the traps that derail HR leaders and how to avoid them.

30-day sprints – a sample 30-day action plan for pulling that specific Employee Experience lever, with simple steps you can test, adapt, and build on right away.

One simple tip – a low-cost, super simple action where you can #DoTheThing *this* week.

Momentum moves – scalable initiatives to make an impact across the enterprise.

Metrics that matter – how to track your progress and prove ROI, reinforcing the core idea that Better Employee Experience (EX) = Better Customer Experience (CX) = Better Business Results.

Using AI to simplify – smart ways to use AI prompts to brainstorm, execute, and measure EX initiatives so you can move with agility, ethically, and efficiently. I recommend ChatGPT or Microsoft Copilot.

Real-world case studies – hear from real companies and thought leaders to inspire you and help you take action, fast.

Learn from Lauren – follow Lauren's story, a mid-career HR leader, someone like you, using this playbook, learning, testing, doing the thing, and making positive change. Learn from Lauren's triumphs and mistakes every step of the way.

To make this a multisensory learning experience through reading, listening, and hands-on exercises, you'll also find journal prompts, choose-your-own-adventure surprises at the end of each chapter, and QR codes linking to bonus tools and special episodes of *The Simplifiers Podcast* to help solidify what you're learning on the go.

Ultimately, *Squash the Sunday Scaries* is a simplified, action-packed playbook that helps HR leaders trade burnout for belonging, confusion for clarity, and workplace dread for a culture people can believe in again.

So, let's meet Lauren, your mirror for this journey.

She's smart, seasoned, and exactly where most HR professionals, like you, find themselves these days: fighting fire drills left, right, and center, fully accountable for culture, and without a clear playbook... until now.

LEARN FROM LAUREN

Oh, Lauren—I feel you, girl...

"Fix culture by Q3."

That's the entire email from the CEO. No brief. No budget. Just a deadline and a blinking cursor. Lauren exhales, stares at the screen, and mutters, "Cool-cool-cool... totally normal request."

In Monday's exec meeting, she asks for clarity.

"Can we define what 'fixed' looks like?"

The CEO drums his fingers. "People are tired. Morale's down. Just... make it better."

The COO adds, "But whatever you do, don't spook the board. We need quick wins."

Back at her desk, Lauren does what most of us do under pressure: tries everything at once. She drafts a 42-question survey ("Comprehensive!"), schedules listening sessions at quarter-end, when everyone is slammed, and posts a chirpy Slack note: "Your voice matters!" The replies land with an iron thud.

"Is this the same survey we took in March?"

"Will this go into the black hole again?"

An honest DM from a manager lands: "I've got three open roles and a launch. My team is feeling the crunch. What's different this time?"

In a grab for "quick wins," she greenlights a Wellness Wednesday. Smoothies happen. Two engineers grab bananas. Slack roasts the fruit ("We asked for clearer priorities, got potassium"). Oof.

That night, Lauren opens a book a mentor mailed to her with a sticky note: "Start with Chapter 1" and one line stops her: "Listening is a closed loop. Don't ask until you're ready to act, and show it."

The next morning, she walks into the COO's office.

"I need two things," she says. "A tiny budget to ship two fixes in 30 days, and permission to share named owners with dates."

He hesitates. "Public owners?"

"If we want trust, we have to show our work."

She scraps the 42 questions and replaces them with a 7-item pulse focused on clarity, tools, recognition, workload, and trust. She pulls the listening sessions forward, recruits two trained facilitators, and commits out loud to a simple "You Said / We Did / Here's What's Next" update within ten business days. *(Spoiler alert: you'll learn exactly how to do that in Chapter 1.)*

There's still skepticism. A recruiter pulls her aside:

"Are we finally going to stop promising 'flexible work' if Tuesdays are now mandatory in-office?"

"Good point," Lauren says. "Brand follows reality. That's our next move. First, we prove to our employees that we can listen and will act on their feedback."

Did Lauren nail it on the first try? Nope. She overbuilt, mistimed, and nearly mistook a smoothie for a strategy. But then she picked the next right action, and **she did the thing.** That's the work.

Hands on the wheel, Lauren makes the first move: Listening with the Intent to Act.

What your workforce really wants

At the core, most employees want three things:

Meaning and purpose
They want their work to matter. No matter their role or level, people want to feel like they're contributing to something bigger than themselves.

To be valued
They want to know their manager and organization see their effort, appreciate their contributions, and respect the insights they bring.

To belong
They want to feel like they belong in the culture, community, and day-to-day experience of your organization.

And yes, of course, they want a steady paycheck, too.

By applying the tools in this book, you'll help your workforce meet these core needs over time.

My promise to you

If you apply the tools in this playbook, your workplace will become more connected, more productive, and more resilient. Change seems to be the only constant in this uncertain economy. That's a given.

Therefore, take The Simplifiers Employee Experience Flywheel (check it out on the back cover!) as your own ~~secret weapon~~ personal compass to help you build a better employee experience for your workforce.

If you implement these best practices with consistency, transparency, and authenticity, what you'll find is that over time, trust grows. Performance follows.

Teams move from Sunday dread to Monday momentum.

And you, as an HR people leader, will find renewed meaning in helping others around you thrive and, ultimately, making a positive impact in the world.

Look, I promise that this book is a quick, practical read for busy HR professionals like you, not a textbook or theory-heavy manual. It's conversational, real, and immediately useful. Just flip to the chapter you need now.

So let's turn the page and put your flywheel in motion, starting where momentum begins: Employee listening that leads to action.

Are you ready? Let's dive in. It's time to simplify: **Employee Listening—Listening with the Intent to Act.**

Choose-your-own-adventure

- Want to get centered before you dive in? Head to page 275.
- Ready to take action? Turn to the next page.

EMPLOYEE LISTENING

1

Employee Listening with the Intent to Act

"If people seem checked out, look closer.
Disengagement is often a response, not a personality trait."

—Mary

The First Turn Of The Flywheel

After the most recent round of layoffs, Lauren inherits three overlapping "engagement" surveys, two anonymous forms, and a Slack channel that functions mostly as a vent board. Participation is high. Follow-through from senior leadership is at an all-time low.

She sketches a plan, then rushes it. The first pulse she drafts has 18 questions and a heavy dose of HR jargon.

A product manager pings her:

"Lauren… love the effort, but this reads like a grad school exam. I've got seven minutes before my next stand-up."

"Fair," she replies, wincing.

She cuts it down to 7 high-signal items, clarity, tools, recognition, workload, and trust. Then she deletes all the buzzwords.

Mistake #2 arrives by calendar invite. She books listening sessions at 4 p.m. on a Friday. Warehouse supervisors write back immediately:

"Shift changes at 3:30. We can't make that."

"Copy," Lauren says.

She adds morning, lunch, and evening options, rotates facilitators, and spells out privacy in plain English.

Before launch, she walks into the COO's office.

"Good news: I don't need more money," Lauren says. "However, I do need three things: system access so we can actually fix what we hear, the authority to greenlight small changes without a committee, and a ten-business-day window to report back publicly."

The COO nods. "Access: yes. Decision rights up to an agreed threshold: yes. Ten days to show progress: do it."

She knows she needs a central place to track ideas, a sort of public backlog. She decides to put it on the company intranet to show her work and create accountability. So she builds a table with columns for:

Idea for Improving EX | Why It Matters | Owner
Action Type | Status | ETA

…and commits to updating it weekly.

Once the survey closes, three pain points jump out: too many meetings, confusing systems, and onboarding that leaves people guessing. Lauren skips the committee route and moves straight to action.

Her first two quick wins are simple: within 30 days, she resets all default meetings to 25 or 50 minutes, adds a one-page agenda template, and introduces an "Is this a meeting or an email?" check. She also launches a single "How do I...?" intranet entry point so employees can find the right policy or request in two clicks or less. Then she tests a 60-day pilot with the Product team, using anchor-day norms with Tuesday and Thursday set aside for collaboration and focused remote days otherwise.

Exactly eight business days after the pulse survey closes, she publishes a one-page:

You Said → We Did → Here's What's Next

…with names and dates, and a little help from AI. A frontline supervisor replies:

"Thanks for putting names on decisions. I can finally explain this to my team."

Trust nudges forward, not from a slogan, but from a calendar invite, a checklist, and two shipped fixes. *Atta girl, Lauren!*

Employee Listening

"Listening counts only when it changes what Monday feels like for your workers."

What it is, simplified.

A five-phase closed-loop system that turns employee input into visible action:

Collect → Interpret → Action Plan → Do The Thing → Report Back

Repeat after me: The magic isn't the data. It's the motion.

What Employee Listening *really* means

Before you ask your workforce what's broken, make sure you're ready to take that feedback and put it into motion. Effective Employee Listening isn't a quarterly questionnaire. It's how your organization learns and demonstrates respect.

Done well, listening can:
- bring to light the friction you can actually fix
- clarify employee and employer expectations and help you decide trade-offs
- rebuild psychological safety through responsiveness
- create a shared backlog of improvements leaders can steward

When people see themes become actions… Momentum compounds.

The five components of closed loop listening

1. Collect

Use a small portfolio of methods to hear real experiences:

- focused pulse surveys (quarterly is plenty) with 7–12 high-signal questions
- listening sessions (facilitated, cross-functional small groups)
- stay interviews (why people remain; what would make them leave)
- open-door hours (leader "Ask Me Anything" blocks, virtual or in person)
- asynchronous channels (an anonymous form plus a named ideas board)

2. Interpret

Synthesize employee feedback with purpose:

- cluster themes (3–7, not 37)
- rate severity (how painful) and determine reach (how many are affected)
- tag each theme to the right EX Flywheel category and subtheme so you can route action clearly and report progress in language that your leaders understand
- identify owners (who is accountable for fixing it)

3. Action Plan

Turn what you heard into a clear, workable plan:

- build the plan and map the milestone tasks
- assign owners and gain buy-in
- allocate resources
- mitigate risks

4. Do The Thing

Turn the plan into visible action:

- deliver quick wins (do now, ≤30 days)
- run experiments (pilot in one team or region with clear exit criteria)
- scope systemic fixes (cross-functional changes with a plan)

5. Tell People

Close the loop by showing what changes, what's next, and who owns it:

- publish "You Said / We Did / Here's What's Next" within 19 business days of closing feedback
- assign names and dates to items in a public backlog
- share monthly progress, especially the "no-for-now" items and the why behind them
- repeat on a predictable cadence so trust can build over time

Why it matters now

In an era of uncertainty, silence after a survey kills trust. Employees don't need perfect answers. They need proof you heard them and a clear plan for what happens next, and by when. But remember:

Listening is a closed loop. Don't ask until you're ready to act, and show it.

Trust is pattern recognition: Say → Do → Repeat

In practice, that looks like:

You Said → We Did → Here's What's Next.

If people speak up and see no visible changes, they learn their voice <u>doesn't</u> matter. And that spreads fast. Remember, you don't have to fix everything. Ship a few meaningful wins quickly and keep showing progress over time. That's the pattern worth recognizing.

Common mistakes & pitfalls (so you can avoid them)

Frequency isn't a strategy. Follow-through is.

Action beats frequency, and silence after listening kills trust. Here are the missteps you'll want to avoid:

Mistake	Solution
Too many surveys; too little action.	Show visible changes. Publish "You Said / We Did / Here's What's Next" with owners and dates.
Vanity metrics. High participation with no behavior change is noise.	Track outcomes (e.g., time-to-first-action, items closed) not just response rates.
No owners. "We're looking into it" is organizational limbo.	Assign a single accountable owner per theme with an ETA and status.
Overpromising.	If you can't deliver now, say so—and state what must be true to revisit it (with a review date).
Treating anonymity as a shield for avoiding hard conversations.	Use anonymity to enable candor, then show up live to address themes and next steps.
Confusing catharsis with progress.	Listening sessions without clear next steps breed cynicism and further distrust. Require every session to end with 1-2 concrete next actions and who owns them.
Collecting names without consent.	Protect privacy: never "out" a commenter.
Fixating on scores instead of stories.	Numbers flag *where* to look; stories reveal *what to do*.

Don't ask for input without budget to act—nothing breaks trust faster.

 Before you implement any Employee Listening strategy, make sure your budget, resources, and headcount are approved and allocated by senior leadership. That way, you can take action quickly once survey results come in and you've identified your quick wins and longer-term priorities.

I'll say it again because it's worth repeating: surveying your people and then doing nothing is one of the fastest ways to further erode trust in senior leadership.

Honestly, it's almost better **not** to conduct Employee Listening at all unless you're truly ready to hear the good, the bad, and the ugly, and then do something about it.

One simple tip — #DoTheThing (this week)

Listen. Gain your quick wins. Tell people.

- Publish a one-page "You Said / We Did / Here's What's Next" within 19 business days of any Employee Listening effort.
- Clearly name who owns each next step.
- Give clear dates for what will happen next.
- If something is a "no-for-now," explain why and what would need to change.
- Consider using ChatGPT or Microsoft Copilot to draft the first version to help you get the ball rolling.

The statements that give you real insights
Pulse survey statements (pick 7–12 max):

___ I know what's expected of me this quarter.

___ I have the tools and information I need to do my job well.

___ My manager gives me actionable feedback when I need it.

___ When I speak up, someone follows up.

___ I received meaningful recognition in the last two weeks.

___ I can see how my work connects to company priorities.

___ My manager helps remove roadblocks so I can accomplish what's expected of me this quarter.

___ I feel like I belong on this team.

___ I trust senior leadership to be transparent about changes.

___ My workload is sustainable most weeks.

___ My manager supports my professional development and advocates for my growth.

___ I feel safe speaking up about problems or mistakes without fear of negative consequences.

___ I receive timely, clear communication about changes that affect my work.

___ Teams across functions collaborate effectively to deliver on shared goals.

___ Decisions that affect my work are made and communicated quickly, with clear ownership.

___ I have the flexibility I need in my time, location, and schedule to do my best work while managing life outside of work.

___ People here are held accountable for living our shared company values.

___ The digital tools and systems I use are intuitive and rarely get in the way of my work.

___ Recognition at our company is fair and inclusive.

___ I would recommend this organization as a place to work.

Use a standard 5-point Likert scale:

1 = STRONGLY DISAGREE	**4** = AGREE
2 = DISAGREE	**5** = STRONGLY AGREE
3 = NEITHER AGREE NOR DISAGREE	

Quick tips:

- ★ Add an optional N/A or "Don't know" response so people aren't forced to guess.
- ★ Report Top-2 Box (4–5) as favorable and Bottom-2 Box (1–2) as unfavorable, then track the median.
- ★ Keep all items positively worded. Avoid reverse-scored phrasing to reduce confusion.

Listening session starters:

- *What's one friction point that slows your work down every week?*
- *If we could fix one thing in 30 days, what should it be, and why?*
- *Where are expectations unclear?*
- *Where are we asking for heroics instead of designing better systems?*
- *What do you need more or less of right now, in order to do your job well?*

Stay interview prompts (30 minutes):

- *What keeps you here?*
- *What might tempt you away?*
- *What's one strength you want to use more often?*
- *What's one blocker I can help remove?*
- *What should I ask you that I haven't?*

Facilitator open & close scripts

- **Open (2 minutes):**
  "Thank you for being here. We value your time and your insights, especially your perspective on where things could work better. This session is for learning. We're capturing themes, not names. Within 19 business days, we'll summarize what we heard and share what happens next: what we'll fix now, what we'll pilot, and what we can't do yet, and why. Your candor helps us to improve the employee experience at work for you and your team."

- **Close (1 minute):**
  "Here's what I heard today: [theme A], [theme B], [theme C]. Did I get that right? If so, we'll confirm these themes in the summary, publish owners and dates, clarify what we can act on now, and circle back within 19 business days with our next steps. Thank you for trusting us with the specifics. We promise to honor that trust by showing progress."

Choose your pace: a 30-day accelerated sprint or a 90-day full sprint.

All "days" below refer to business days (Monday–Friday). Pick 30 business days for speed. Pick 90 for a quarterly rhythm.

Option one: Designing your 30-day accelerated employee listening sprint

Goal: Deliver visible trust wins in 30 business days by collecting focused feedback, acting on 2–3 high-impact issues, and locking in a repeatable close-the-loop cadence.

Day 1–2: Kickoff and framing

- The CEO or executive sponsor sends the "why" and "what's different" note.
- Publish the listening charter (purpose, confidentiality, cadence).
- Open the "Idea to Try" channel for named submissions.
- Schedule the "Report Back" communication to go out on business Day 19.

Day 3–5: Pulse is live (keep it to 10 items)

- Keep the survey open for a three-business-day window and send two reminders.
- Target segments by role, location, and level (no cuts below N=5).

Day 6–9: Listening sessions (high-signal, not high-volume)

- Hold 4–6 sessions, 45 minutes each, across morning, lunch, and evening time slots with a cross-functional mix.
- Run one stay interview block with 10–12 people for 20–30 minutes each, using a shared script.
- Have facilitators capture theme snippets, not names.

Day 10–12: Interpret and prioritize

- Triage team clusters 3–5 themes using severity × reach.
- For each theme, assign an owner, one success outcome, one quick win, and one pilot.

Day 13–18: Ship quick wins and launch one pilot

- Quick win example: default 25- and 50-minute meetings plus a one-page agenda template.
- Quick win example: a "How do I...?" intranet entry point that routes employees to the right form or policy.
- Pilot example: anchor-day norms in one team, with exit criteria and a decision date.
- The executive sponsor meets twice to unblock progress.

Day 19–20: Close the loop (version 1)

- Publish "You Said / We Did / Here's What's Next" in a one-page update with names and dates.
- Managers receive a one-minute script to cascade in team huddles and 1:1s.

Day 21–26: Sustain and show progress

- Track adoption of quick wins (e.g., percentage of meetings using the agenda template; intranet click-throughs).
- Conduct a midpoint pilot check and adjust.

Day 27–30: Wrap, decide, and reset

- Decide whether the pilot should continue, expand, or stop, then post the results to the backlog.
- Share a 30-business-day summary slide at the next all-hands meeting: participation, time-to-first-action, theme-to-action conversion, and one story.
- Announce the next 30-day sprint, including one new theme and whether the pilot will continue.

Option two: Designing your 90-day extended employee listening sprint

Goal: Show visible progress on a few high-impact issues to rebuild trust and establish a quarterly listening cadence.

Week 1–2: Focus and setup

- Consolidate overlapping employee feedback channels into one quarterly pulse survey and monthly roundtables.
- Draft a listening charter outlining purpose, methods, confidentiality, and cadence.
- Stand up a public backlog, a shared board or page that makes employee feedback and follow-through visible. Include these fields: Theme, Impact, Owner, Action Type (quick win, experiment, or systemic fix), Status, ETA.
- Identify a small team to review and prioritize the top themes with you, made up of People Ops, one executive, and two cross-functional leaders.

- Prepare manager talking points on the "why" and "what's different now."

Week 3–4: Collect insights (light and high-signal)

- Launch a pulse survey with 8–12 items covering clarity of expectations, manager support, tool friction, recognition, belonging, workload, and trust in senior leadership.
- Hold listening sessions with cross-functional groups for 60 minutes each, using two facilitators: one to guide the discussion and one to capture insights. If appropriate and permitted by your company's privacy guidelines, use AI to record and transcribe the session so you can review themes more accurately afterward.
- Conduct stay interviews lasting 30 minutes each, using five common questions to better understand why people stay at your organization.
- Add an asynchronous "Idea to Try" channel with a simple prompt: *If we could fix one thing in 30 days, what should it be, and why?*

Week 5–6: Interpret and prioritize

- Cluster the top 3–5 themes using severity × reach.
- Pair each theme with a named owner and one success outcome (e.g., "Reduce meeting time by 15% in 60 days").
- Identify one quick win per theme, one pilot to test, and the metrics or KPIs you'll track to measure success.

Week 7–8: Act (quick wins and one pilot)

- Implement two quick wins during this phase.
- Launch one pilot with exit criteria and a decision date.
- Unblock owners through weekly leadership check-ins.

Week 9–10: Report back and reset

- Publish "You Said / We Did / Here's What's Next."
- Close the loop in the places your workforce already looks for information and updates: all-hands meetings, the intranet, their manager 1:1 talking points, and the internal channels they trust most.
- Plan the next sprint with one new theme and one continuing pilot.

Using AI to simplify (Employee Listening)

Here are copy-and-paste-ready prompts you can drop into ChatGPT or another generative AI tool, such as Microsoft Copilot or Gemini. Each "even better" version adds context, tone, ethics, and structure so the output is safer and more useful.

Use Case	Good Prompt	Even Better Prompt
Theme clustering (open-text comments)	"Cluster these survey comments into themes."	"You are an HR analyst. Review the anonymized employee comments below and group them into 3–7 themes. For each theme, provide: a short name, a one-sentence description, paraphrased examples, and a reach × severity estimate (Low/Medium/High). Do not include names or direct quotes. Flag any potentially sensitive topics for human review. Return the results as a table. Comments: [paste comments here]"
Draft 'You Said / We Did / Here's What's Next'	"Write a summary of what we heard and next steps."	"Draft a one-page 'You Said / We Did / Here's What's Next' update for employees. Tone: clear, respectful, and free of spin. Do not include any personally identifiable information, and do not make promises we can't keep. Include: 1) the top three themes in plain English, 2) what we've already shipped, including the owner and date, 3) what's next, including the owner and target date, and 4) any 'no-for-now' items, along with the reason why and when they will be reviewed again. Return the draft with clear headings. Here are the facts to use: [paste your bullet list of actions and themes here]"
Facilitator guide for listening sessions	"Create questions for an Employee Listening session."	"Create a 45-minute facilitation guide for an Employee Listening session. The audience is a cross-functional group of employees. The goals are to surface friction points and avoid blame. Include: an opening script that explains privacy and purpose, six discussion questions that move from concrete to reflective, suggested time blocks for each section, de-biasing tips for the facilitator, and a two-minute closing script that sets the expectation for a follow-up within 19 business days. Tone: neutral, curious, and trauma-informed. Return the guide in a clear, easy-to-use format."

Manager 1:1 prompt kit (post-survey)	"Give me 1:1 questions about survey results."	"Create a one-page manager 1:1 discussion guide to help managers talk about pulse survey results without becoming defensive. Include: four opening lines, six discussion questions tied to these themes [paste themes here], a four-step mini-script using this flow—Acknowledge → Explore → Align → Act—and a five-sentence recap template managers can use afterward. Avoid jargon and keep the language clear and concise."
Translation (human review required)	"Translate this into Spanish."	"Translate the employee update below into [insert language] at a ninth-grade reading level. Keep the tone respectful, clear, and plain. Do not translate product codenames. Then provide: 1) the translated version, 2) a list of any idioms or phrases you localized, and 3) any cultural or wording risks a human reviewer should check before sending. Here is the message: [paste message here]"
Backlog builder (owners & ETAs)	"Turn these ideas into a backlog."	"Turn the items below into a public Employee Experience (EX) backlog. Use these columns: Theme, Why It Matters (12 words or fewer), Owner (role), Action Type (Quick Win, Pilot, or Systemic Fix), Status (Planned, In Progress, Complete, On Hold, or No for Now), ETA, and Last Update Note. Use today's date where needed. If an owner or ETA is missing, suggest one based on the theme. For any item marked 'No for Now,' include a brief explanation in the Last Update Note. Return the results as a table. Here are the items: [paste list here]"
Bias & privacy check (safety pass)	"Check this draft for issues."	"Review the draft below for privacy and bias risks. 1) Highlight any personal data, health information, or identifying details, and suggest how to anonymize them. 2) Flag any language that could stigmatize individuals or groups, and offer more neutral alternatives. 3) Note any over-promises or timelines that should be softened before this is shared. Return your review as a three-section checklist with suggested edits. Here is the draft: [paste draft here]"

Quick AI guardrails reminder:

- Strip names, teams with fewer than five people, and any personally identifiable information (PII) including employee's first and last names and employee ID number, before pasting into AI.
- Treat outputs as what I call "dirty first drafts." They always require a human to read, review, proofread, and own the final wording and decisions.
- Log what AI touched for transparency, and keep access to raw comments limited.

Routing & accountability (so actions don't stall)

- Assign a single accountable owner to each theme, including name and title.
- Use a simple RACI for each theme:

  » **Responsible** (who does the work)
  » **Accountable** (who signs off; their name is on the line)
  » **Consulted** (who the impacted teams are)
  » **Informed** (your stakeholders)

- Create clear service levels:

  » Acknowledge new items within 5 business days.
  » Make a decision or define the next step within 15 business days.
  » Show first visible progress within 30 days, or communicate why not.

- Review the backlog weekly at the executive stand-up. Spend 10 minutes unblocking owners.

Sample routing cheat sheet

Domain Tag	Routes To	Owner(s)
Employer Branding	→	Talent Acquisition, People Ops, Marketing, and Internal Communications
Leadership Development	→	Learning and Development, People Ops, and Business Unit Leaders
Succession Planning	→	People Ops, Talent Management, Executive Leadership, and Business Unit Leaders
Recognition + Engagement	→	People Ops, Internal Communications, and Site or Event Leads
New Hire Onboarding	→	Talent Acquisition, People Ops, Learning and Development, Hiring Managers
Digital Employee Experience (DEX)	→	IT, People Ops, Operations, and Internal Systems Owners
Workplace Experience	→	Facilities, Operations, People Ops, and Site Leaders
The People Leader's Playbook (Manager Enablement)	→	People Ops, Learning and Development, and People Managers

Public backlog fields:

Idea for Improving EX | Why It Matters | Owner | Action Type | Status | ETA | Last update link | EX Flywheel Category

Creating safe spaces to speak up

To gain a full picture of what's broken and where there's opportunity to improve, you need to make sure all employees have a confidential way to share feedback and feel safe speaking up.

Here's how.

- Segment your listening by function, location, level, and identity groups where appropriate to ensure underheard voices are included. Use privacy thresholds to avoid identifiability.
- Vary the format, such as spoken or written, live or asynchronous, and on-hours or off-hours, so people with different comfort levels and schedules can participate. This is especially important for front-line and international employees working across time zones.
- Rotate facilitators and session times to broaden access.
- Offer closed captioning, multilingual options, and written channels to reduce barriers.
- Compensate employee resource groups (ERGs) and affinity groups for participating in listening efforts, such as protected time or stipends for future ERG programming, to avoid invisible labor.

What to do when the answer is a "no for now"

Sometimes the top theme is something you simply can't change right now, such as wage structure, a four-day workweek, or an office lease. When that happens, resist the urge to go silent.

Instead, follow this hard-no playbook to show courage, not spin:

- **Name the constraint.** ("Our current client service level agreements, or SLAs, require...")
- **Explain the path to yes.** ("To revisit this, we need X, Y, and Z to be true.")
- **Offer a proxy improvement.** ("Meanwhile, we're piloting A and B to improve things..")
- **Set a review date.** ("We'll reassess in 90 days and report back.")

Use this playbook to build your customized "It's a no for now, and here's why" communication before sending it out. Respect grows when you tell the truth and still look for relief valves that move people one step closer to yes.

Momentum moves
(from quick wins to lasting change)

90-day listening plan (template)

- **Objectives:** For example, reduce meeting time by 15% and improve "I know what's expected" by 10 points.
- **Methods:** One pulse survey, three listening sessions, and 10 stay interviews.
- **Themes and owners:** List each theme with its RACI.
- **Actions:** Two quick wins, one pilot, and one scoped systemic fix.
- **Communication:** Include the date and channels for your "You Said / We Did / Here's What's Next" update.
- **Metrics:** Baseline, target, and review date.

Public backlog

Make the work visible. Every item should have a human owner and an ETA. Keep closed items visible for 90 days to show progress.

Manager Listening Kit

Include a 1:1 question bank, a stay interview guide, guidance on how to escalate a theme, and tips for closing the loop at the team level. Add a five-sentence recognition script and a one-paragraph "no for now" explanation template. Don't forget: AI can help you build a first draft for all of this!

Community of Practice for facilitators

Train a handful of internal facilitators. Provide scripts, timers, de-biasing tips, and a 15-minute debrief ritual. Rotate pairings to prevent groupthink.

Quarterly "Listening to Action" review (30 minutes)

Have senior leaders review closed items, unblock stuck ones, and choose priorities for the next sprint. Share one story about a time when listening changed a decision.

METRICS THAT MATTER

Employee Listening Metrics	What It Tells You
Participation rate (by org, by segment)	How many employees are engaging in the listening effort, and where response rates are strong or weak across the organization.
Theme-to-action conversion	Whether the top themes raised by employees are being translated into visible action with active owners and next steps.
Time-to-first-action	How quickly the organization moves from collecting feedback to taking the first visible step. How many business days?
Resolution rate	How many items are being closed versus opened in each sprint, which helps show progress over time.
Sentiment shift	Whether employee perception is improving on key trust signals, such as "When I speak up, someone follows up."
Manager-level metrics	Whether managers are reinforcing the listening process locally through behaviors like completing 1:1s and closing the loop with their teams.

Pick three metrics to report every month. Consistency compounds.

One slide, one message, one call to action.
Make the win obvious.

Example monthly report (one slide):
- Participation: 71% (up 6 points)
- Theme-to-action conversion: 4/5 (new owners assigned)
- Time-to-first-action: 9 business days (target: 10 or fewer)

In this sprint, we completed six items: meeting hygiene, intranet entry point, day-one manager checklist, and more.

Here's what's next: expand the anchor-day pilot and scope a systemic fix for tool access.

Keep your slide visually appealing, easy to digest, and centered on the top message and call to action your senior executives need to understand about this EX initiative.

Keep it concise, compelling, and *simple* to understand.

Sample internal communications scripts & simplified tools

Closing the loop (one paragraph):

"You said our meetings often lack outcomes and run long, that new hires struggle to find information in week one, and that tool access is confusing. We did three things: (1) set default 25/50-minute meetings with a shared agenda template; (2) launched a single 'How do I...?' intranet entry point; (3) created a day-one checklist for managers. Here's what's next: piloting 'anchor-day' collaboration norms in Product through Q2. Owners: Jordan (IT), Priya (People Ops), Marcus (Product)."

No-for-now explanation (two sentences):

"We can't move to a four-day workweek this quarter due to client SLAs and current staffing. We'll revisit in six months after we complete a staffing model and client consultation."

Here's the template - fill-in-the-blanks:

We can't do this suggested solution due to this exact reason. We'll revisit in this exact amount of time after we complete this specific action item that will bring us more data to consider when deciding to action this suggested solution.

Manager 1:1 listening agenda (25 minutes):

- Wins worth celebrating since last week (5 minutes)
- Roadblocks I can help clear for you (5 minutes)
- Priorities for this week ahead (10 minutes)
- One improvement idea to consider (5 minutes)

REAL-WORLD CASE STUDY

Listening That Builds Trust, Even When the Answer Is No

Employee listening only works when leaders are prepared to act on what they hear, or clearly explain why they cannot.

Steve Cadigan, Author, Talent Strategist, and LinkedIn's first CHRO, learned this lesson firsthand during a period of intense hypergrowth. As LinkedIn rapidly doubled its employee population, offices, countries, and revenue, inevitable complexity followed. New leaders were managing larger teams, new processes were being built on the fly, and physical distance grew between the front line and senior leadership as offices expanded across geographies.

Steve, the CEO, and the executive team recognized that this moment required more than speed. It required intentional communication, strong signal carry, and clear pathways for employees to have a voice.

As the company scaled, rumors and myths with little basis in fact began to surface. Employees felt increasingly disconnected compared to when the organization was smaller, communication channels were easier to navigate, and leaders were more visible and accessible.

The Challenge: Feedback Without Follow-Through Breeds Mistrust

Rather than dismissing concerns, Steve and the CEO chose to listen directly. They launched listening tours across teams and geographies and shifted employee surveys from once a year to every six months, centered on two simple questions:

- What is working well that we should protect?
- What one or two things are not working that we need to address?

The approach surfaced real issues, but it also revealed something else. Employees wanted proof that leadership was actually hearing them.

The Strategy: Close the Loop With Evidence, Not Spin

One survey result presented both a challenge and an opportunity.

Employees based in San Francisco asked for a company shuttle between the city and LinkedIn headquarters in Mountain View. The request appeared frequently in engagement data and reflected a real pain point. Long commutes meant less time with family and friends. Instead of ignoring the request or issuing a quick "no," Steve did the research.

The findings mattered. Only a small minority of employees lived in San Francisco, and the cost of running shuttles twice daily would exceed a quarter of a million dollars annually. Nearby tech companies would not allow shuttle sharing due to confidentiality concerns.

When Steve presented these facts in a town hall, he did not dictate a decision. He asked employees whether this was the best use of company money, or not.

They said no.

The Outcome: Trust Increased, Even When the Decision Was "No"

The result was trust.

Employees appreciated that leadership listened, investigated the request seriously, and explained the decision transparently. Even without getting what they asked for, they felt respected. Closing the loop mattered more than the outcome itself.

Steve's takeaway is simple. Listening is not about saying yes to everything. It is about replacing anecdotes with evidence, myths with facts, and silence with clarity. When leaders consistently listen, communicate back, and explain their decisions, employees stay engaged even during uncertainty.

That is listening with the intent to act.

Practical Lessons for HR and People Leaders

- Listening without follow-through erodes trust. Close the loop every time, even when the answer is "no."
- Evidence beats anecdotes. Research requests before deciding, then share the facts openly.
- Transparency matters more than outcomes. People can accept "no" when they understand the why.

In the end, transparency builds trust. Even a "no" works when people understand why.

The 7-minute reality check (Employee Listening)

Open your last survey deck and your top Slack or help desk threads. Set a timer for seven minutes* and journal it out. Be blunt. Remember, speed beats spin.

1. **Where do employees most often say, *"I've told them this before, and nothing changes"*? What would closing the loop look like there?**

2. **Which three questions will you ask every quarter, without fail, and why those three?**

3. **What is one quick win you can ship in 14 days to signal that you're serious and actually listening?**

4. **Who will be the named owner for your top theme, and what support do they need?**

5. **What will you stop measuring so you can pay attention to what matters?**

Bottom line: Listening only counts when people can see what changed, with a name and a date.

Ok, I have to introduce you to the magic of a seven minute timer! This is a Simplifier secret!

Anytime you feel stuck, set a timer for seven minutes and start journaling. You'll find the first couple of minutes are challenging, but just put pen to paper and begin. Then, when you get into the flow, your brain clicks into action, and BOOM. You'll have clarity in no time at all.

Will you solve everything? No. But I guarantee you'll make forward progress, every single time. Try it!

Trust is earned through effective listening, taking action, and telling people about it, all along the way.

Remember: trust doesn't snap in one dramatic moment. It slowly frays with every mismatch between the internal message being communicated and how your employees actually feel on Monday morning.

Always zoom out and look at the bigger picture.

Ask yourself:

- What did we learn in this phase of Employee Listening?
- What are most workers, teams, or departments saying is broken right now?
- Where is the best opportunity to act first, either as a quick win or a larger initiative?

JOT DOWN YOUR IDEAS HERE

FIND BONUS RESOURCES HERE

Choose-your-own-adventure

- Feeling overwhelmed? Head to page 278.
- Looking for a bit of clarity on where to go next? Study the flywheel on the back cover and then choose the chapter you need most.
- If it's talent assessments, head to page 75.
- If it's leadership development, head to page 95.
- If it's succession planning, head to page 117.
- If it's recognition + engagement, head to page 135.
- If it's new hire onboarding, head to page 155.
- If it's the digital employee experience, head to page 175.
- If it's workplace experience, head to page 193.
- If it's your managers and people leaders, head to page 217.
- If it's your employer brand, head to the next chapter.

You've listened. You've acted. Now we move to the bridge between what employees live and what the outside world hears: your employer brand.

If listening is the heartbeat, brand is the PA system. It broadcasts promises, so they'd better match the rhythm inside the building. When the career site proclaims, "We trust you to work where you work best," but calendars are filled with surprise in-office mandates and 8 a.m. all-hands meetings, that's not branding. *That's a breach of trust.*

This next chapter is about truth in advertising for work.

We'll align your Employer Value Proposition (EVP) with lived reality, swapping spin for receipts, and evolving the "You Said / We Did / Here's What's Next" framework into a "We Said / We Do" ethos that sits proudly on your career site.

Because when the story you tell on the outside matches what people experience on the inside, you don't just recruit better. You retain better, perform better, and give your managers something rare in a noisy world: authentic credibility.

Are you ready?

Let's dive in.

It's time to simplify: **Employer Branding That Matches the Inside.**

EMPLOYER BRANDING

2

Employer Branding That Matches the Inside

"If the inside story does not match the outside promise, people notice."

—Mary

The "words vs. Mondays" moment

"Flexible work. Rapid growth. Work-life balance."

That's what the career page promises. Lauren scrolls, then glances at her calendar: three surprise "mandatory in-office" meetings this week and a Friday 7:30 a.m. all-hands. She winces.

In the executive check-in, she musters the courage and asks, "Do we truly offer flexibility?"

The COO says, "Mostly. Our team leaders decide."

A recruiter messages Lauren privately: "Can I be frank with you? Our candidates keep asking what 'flexible' actually means. I skirt the question most days. Then they quit three months in."

Lauren makes two early mistakes:

- She drafts shiny new "guiding principles" copy before checking it against workplace reality. Marketing loves it, but the managers don't recognize it.
- She trains recruiters on the new talk track but forgets to brief the hiring managers. Whoops. The result? Interviews go off-script fast, leaving candidates puzzled.

She quickly realizes that she needs to course-correct using this chapter's playbook:

- **Audit first, rewrite second.** She maps promises versus proof across the entire employee journey.
- **Right-size the language.** "Flexible work" becomes, "Two anchor days on-site (Tuesdays and Thursdays). Remote otherwise, with manager-approved exceptions," after confirming that it's true across job levels and departments.
- **Align the system.** She runs a 60-minute sync with recruiters and hiring managers to lock in expectation-setting scripts, then secures executive leadership team (ELT) agreement on a quarterly employer value proposition (EVP) Now → Next review with owners, dates, and receipts.

Two weeks later, a candidate says after onboarding, "This is exactly what they described."

Eye-rolls in town halls taper off. Credibility clicks.

"Hey, hey, we're getting somewhere now," she thinks.

Employer Branding

"What you say your company is versus what it actually is like working there could be two very different things. The wheels might be coming off the bus right from the jump if you're overpromising and underdelivering."

What it is, simplified.

Your employer brand is the promise you make to candidates and employees about what it's like to work here. Your EVP (Employer Value Proposition) is the specific deal behind that promise: the give versus the get.

- What people can expect: growth, flexibility, fair pay, meaningful work.
- What the organization expects in return: outcomes, behaviors, values.

The job is simple: make the promise match what Monday actually feels like.

Then show your receipts with clear behaviors, policies, and proof points that back it up. That's how you start to squash the Sunday Scaries.

Why it matters now

Your company's brand isn't the sizzle reel on your careers page. It's the gap between what you promise and what people actually experience at work. When you say "flexible work" but stack surprise mandates, or preach "high trust" while requiring five approvals for a pen, candidates notice, new hires feel duped, and bad Glassdoor reviews pile up.

Close the gap and you reduce attrition, bad-fit hires, and onboarding buyer's remorse, while lifting time to productivity and referral rates.

Leave it open and trust bleeds out. Managers spend their weeks in damage control, and the brand starts paying a quiet tax in churn, disengagement, and customers who feel the cold shoulder too.

Common mistakes & pitfalls (so you can avoid them)

There's nothing wrong with having aspirations for what you want the culture at your organization to look and feel like. In fact, that's what the Now → Next framework (see page 61) is all about: casting a vision for a thriving culture and creating a repeatable, scalable plan to build it.

However, if your company isn't there yet, is it fair to say that's what your organization is known for if it's not the reality? I don't think so.

Instead, this is an incremental process. You take steady steps toward improvement over time. Here are some other mistakes to avoid:

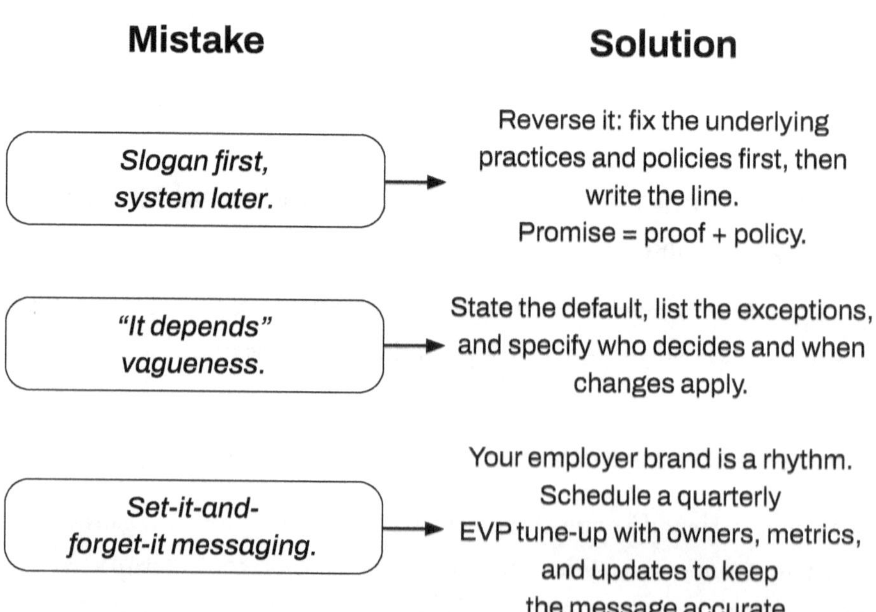

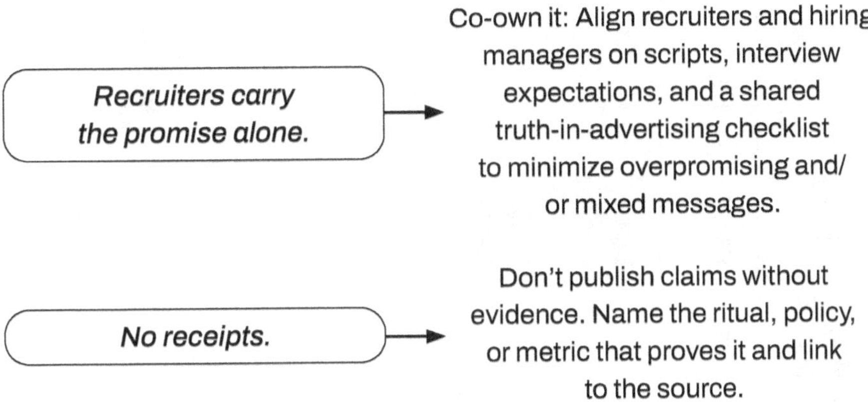

EVP alignment, simplified.

Step 1: Audit Your Touchpoints.

Words → Behaviors → Proof

What this is: a fast scan of every place you make a promise, then a check on whether the culture actually matches it.

How to use it: Fill the grid with specifics, flag the gaps, and assign an owner and a date. If there's no receipt, it's a risk.

Create your own skim-friendly grid similar to this:

Touchpoint	The Promise (Exact Words)	The Lived Reality (What It Means Today)	Proof/Receipts (Policy, Ritual, Metric)	Owner	Risk Level
Careers site	"Flexible work"	Tuesday/Thursday anchor days and core hours	Hybrid policy, calendar norms, badge data	People Ops	High
Job posts	"Rapid growth"	Two promotion cycles per year; clear bands	Promotion policy, banding document	Comp	Medium
Interview scripts	"High autonomy"	Decisions require one approver	RACI chart, decision SLAs	Hiring Manager	Medium
Offer letter	"Learning culture"	Independent Development Plan (IDP) required; monthly learning labs	IDP adoption %, lab attendance	L&D	Low
Onboarding communications	"Belonging"	Buddies assigned; welcome ritual	Buddy program document; Day 30 NPS (Net Promoter Score)	EX	Medium
Wall slogans/ town hall messaging	"Trust & transparency"	Monthly "You Said / We Did / Here's What's Next"	Backlog URL, cadence dates	ELT	Medium
Newsletters & bulletin boards	"Our focus this quarter"	Revenue targets; stretch goals	Sales tracking reports	ELT	High

Rule: if you can't list a receipt, don't claim the promise.

Step 2: Create a Message Map. (Values → Behaviors → Proof → Language)

What this is: your no-spin translator. It turns value words into things people can see, measure, and say consistently across careers pages, interviews, and onboarding.

How to use it: Pick a company core value, define the observable behavior, name the proof you'll publish, then write the exact sentence you'll use everywhere.

Value	Behavior (observable)	Proof/Receipts	Language (use verbatim)
Trust	Publish decisions with owner and date	"You Said / We Did / Here's What's Next" updates every 30 days	We share decisions with names and dates every month.
Flexibility	Two anchor days in office; no meeting Wednesdays	Handbook policy; calendar analysis showing meeting-light Wednesdays	We work in-office Tuesdays and Thursdays. Wednesdays are meeting-light by design.
Growth	Leadership development focused on quarterly IDP check-ins + micro-assignments	IDP adoption %; number of assignments shipped	Every role has a 90-day growth plan with real projects.

Once aligned by your ELT and key stakeholders, drop this map into your careers page, interview guides, and onboarding.

Step 3: Take Action on Your Remediation Path

Fix the system or fix the sentence. When promise ≠ reality, you've got two honest choices:

Evolve practices to meet the promise (preferred).
Keep the headline, like "flexibility," then operationalize it. Set anchor days, core hours, and meeting norms. Publish them where people can see them.

Time-box it to 30 business days or fewer, name owners, and show receipts: a policy link, calendar analysis, adoption metrics. Measure productivity, revenue targets, or other KPIs against the change.

Right-size the promise to fit reality (honest beats hype).
Rewrite the copy to match today, then add a Now → Next line with a concrete experiment and decision date.

Example: "Two anchor days + core hours; remote otherwise. Next: testing manager-led flex windows in Q3."

Either way, publish Now → Next with owners and dates, then review it quarterly.

Sample Remediation Planner (copy/paste and fill in per promise)

Promise: "Flexible work"
Reality: Unwritten in-office Tuesdays; meetings drift past 5 p.m.
Path Chosen: Fix the system *(or fix the sentence for now)*

Actions:

- Set Tuesday/Thursday anchor days; define core hours as 10 a.m.–3 p.m.
- Make Wednesday meeting-light; update the handbook and team charters

Owner: COO + People Ops

ETA: 30 business days or fewer

Receipts (the proof we'll publish): policy link, calendar audit, adoption %

Now → Next:

Now: Tuesday/Thursday anchor days are live.

Next: Review adoption and exceptions in 60 days.

How to run this (fast and clean)

- Pick three gaps max. Ship those and park the rest in a visible backlog.
- Name a single owner per gap. Create a RACI if you need further clarity, but remember: one name is accountable.
- Publish receipts. Use policy links, calendar audits, adoption metrics, and owner + date on decisions.
- Schedule the check-ins for the year now. Quarterly EVP tune-ups should take 45 minutes to track what changed, what's next, and what copy needs to evolve.

One-liner you can paste on the careers page

"We share what's true now and what's coming next, by name and date, so candidates and employees can trust the path we are headed down, not just the promise."

The Now → Next framework

This framework helps you show where the organization is now versus where it's headed next. Maybe that's the skills certain teams need to develop, or maybe it's a section of the handbook that needs updating. Either way, you look at what is true now and what you want to be true next, then use that framing everywhere you make promises, including your careers site, town hall slides, and internal newsletter.

Now

- What's true today (policy, ritual, metric)
- Who owns it

Next (0–90 days)

- What's changing (pilot or policy)
- ETA + decision date

Receipts: Where to see progress (link to backlog or cadence document)

Example (Flex):

Now:

- Tuesday/Thursday anchor days with core hours 10 a.m.–3 p.m. in their local timezone.
- Owner: COO.

Next (by March 31):

- Trial meeting-light Wednesdays, so employees can focus on "heads-down" work.
- Decision by April 30.

Receipts: Can be found on the intranet or in the EX backlog

30-day employer branding sprint

Days 1–3: Pull the receipts

- Scrape careers copy, job descriptions, interview guides, offer templates, onboarding materials, and town hall slides.
- Gather policy documents and any supporting metrics, such as attendance, IDP adoption, and decision SLAs.

Days 4–6: Reality checks

- Hold three listening huddles with recruiters, managers, and new hires.
- Mark each promise as High, Medium, or Low risk for mismatch.

Days 7–10: Message map + Now → Next

- Convert the top five promises into behaviors + proof.
- Draft Now → Next blurbs. Identify owners and ETAs.

Days 11–15: Align the system

- Hold a 60-minute joint sync with talent acquisition and hiring managers. Lock the scripts.
- Update job description snippets, phone screen scripts, and offer language.

Days 16–20: Publish and train

- Patch careers page sections with receipts + Now → Next.
- Run a 45-minute manager enablement training session on expectation-setting without spin.

Days 21–25: Spot checks

- Listen to five recruiter screening calls and five interviews. Nudge where people go off-script.
- Confirm the onboarding Day 1 deck reflects the changes.

Days 26–30: Report and lock cadence

- Share a "We Said → We Do" slide at the next all-hands meeting with the top three promises, receipts, and next steps.

- Put the Employer Value Proposition (EVP) review on a quarterly Executive Leadership Team (ELT) agenda for 15 minutes, with owners reporting.

One simple tip — #DoTheThing (this week)

Pick one promise on your careers page that makes you sweat a little: "flexible work," "transparent pay," "rapid growth," or anything else that would spark a Slack eye-roll if tested today.

- Add a Now → Next block with a real owner and a real date.
- Publish it where people actually look: your careers page, intranet, and manager notes.
- Then do the part that actually rebuilds trust: hit the date.

Try this 15-minute play:

- **Name the risk:** "Flexible work" is vague and uneven.
- **Write the receipt:**

  » Now: Tuesday/Thursday anchor days + 10 a.m.–3 p.m. core hours.
  » Next: review adoption and exceptions by March 14.
- **Assign a human:** Owner: COO + People Ops.
- **Post it, pin it, say it:** careers site, all-hands slide, manager script.
- **Deliver it, loudly:** close the loop with "We Said / We Did / Here's What's Next."

Copy-paste mini-template:

- **Promise:** "___________________"
- **Now:** _______________________ (owner + live date)
- **Next:** _______________________ (owner + review/decision date)

One line to use in your update:

- *"We're replacing slogans with receipts: names, dates, and progress you can see."*

Using AI to simplify (Employer Branding)

Use Case	Good Prompt	Even Better Prompt
Promise → Proof scanner	"Identify vague claims in this section of copy on our career site."	"Act as an HR brand auditor with 10+ years of experience. Review the careers site copy below and identify any promises that lack receipts. For each one, suggest: 1) a measurable behavior, 2) one proof point (policy, ritual, or metric), and 3) a Now → Next line. Return the results as a table."
Job Description (JD) rewrite	"Rewrite this job description to reflect a hybrid work schedule."	"Rewrite this job description section to reflect our exact hybrid norms: Tuesdays and Thursdays on-site, with core hours from 10 a.m. to 3 p.m. in the local time zone. Keep the tone plain and candidate-friendly. Include one bullet called 'What this means week to week.'"
Interview script	"Create interview questions to assess autonomy."	"Draft five interview questions that assess autonomy fit. Include what a strong answer sounds like in our context, including clear outcomes and decision boundaries."
"We Said / We Did / Here's What's Next"	"Write an update on what we promised."	"Draft a one-slide 'We Said / We Did / Here's What's Next' update with: 1) the top three promises, 2) the receipt for each one, and 3) what's next, including the owner and date. Use bullet points only. No adjectives, just facts."

Quick AI guardrails reminder:

- Strip names and any personally identifiable information (PII) before pasting content into AI.
- Treat outputs from AI as a "dirty first draft." A human should always read, review, proofread, and own the final wording and decisions.
- Use AI to sharpen language, clarify the message, and spot gaps, but it goes without saying, never to invent proof that doesn't exist.
- Publish only what your organization can back up with a real policy, practice, metric, or observable behavior.
- Log what AI touched for transparency, and keep access to source material limited.

METRICS THAT MATTER

Employer Branding Metrics	What It Tells You
Offer-to-Start Retention (Day 0 → Day 1)	Whether accepted offers are actually converting into Day 1 arrivals. If people drop off before they start, your promise likely didn't hold up.
New-Hire NPS (Day 30)	Whether reality matched what was promised during recruiting and hiring. This gives you one of the clearest early signals of employer brand truthfulness.
Regretted Attrition (0–6 / 0–12 months)	Whether high-potential new hires are leaving early because of expectation gaps, onboarding breakdowns, or poor fit. These are the new hires you wish hadn't left.
"Consistency" Mentions (Glassdoor, Indeed, LinkedIn posts)	Whether candidates and former employees describe the experience as matching, or not matching, what the organization promised or felt it was a "bait-and-switch" situation.

Recruiter Rework Rate	How often offers are declined because of expectation mismatch around location, hours, travel, flexibility, and/or role scope.
Time to Confidence (New Hire Day 45)	Whether new hires feel equipped and capable enough to do the job they were hired to do.
Onboarding "Receipts" Completion	Whether teams are posting clear Now → Next commitments with owners and dates in the first 30 days.

Bottom line: If you can't show a number, a date, or a quote from a real new hire, it's not a metric. It's marketing.

REAL-WORLD CASE STUDY

When the Inside Story Matches the Outside Story

When employer branding works, it does more than attract candidates. It helps people understand what they are walking into, what success will require, and whether they will truly belong. That matters because, as **Bryan Chaney, Co-Founder of People Brand Collective and former Vice President, Internal Communications & Talent Brand,** explained, the employer brand is really the organization's experience brand, shaped by what people actually live every day, not just what gets marketed to candidates.

The Challenge: A Promise Out of Sync

At a consumer-facing entertainment company with a global workforce of 1,300+ full-time employees, rapid growth had created real complexity. After multiple acquisitions, the company was trying to bring together people from very different legacy cultures, expectations, and ways of working. But the employer brand had not kept pace. The external story leaned heavily on the consumer brand, while the careers site was outdated and the candidate experience offered very little insight into what employees could actually expect. Internally, values were not yet clear enough to guide behavior in a consistent way. The result was a gap between promise and reality. And when people do not fully understand the exchange they are stepping into, or whether they belong there at all, that is where the Sunday Scaries can begin.

The Strategy: Tell the Truth First

Bryan and the team did not begin with polished messaging. They began with listening. They looked across employee feedback channels, external review sites, internal conversations, and executive perspectives to understand the real experience people were having. That research helped them clarify three core elements of the Employer Value Proposition (EVP):

- The nature and demands of the work itself.
- The qualities of people who succeed there.
- The unique opportunity the company offered in the market.

Just as important, they worked to make the values real.

Bryan said they were aiming for "the output from the values" and how those values mapped to behaviors. Then they took it one step further and mapped those behaviors to actions, asking: "If this value is true, what are the behaviors and actions that actually show up on teams?"

That gave leaders something tangible to point to, hold people accountable for, and build into the way the organization worked. From there, the team embedded those ideas into recruiter enablement, interview questions, performance management, and other people practices so the story being told would better match the experience people would actually have.

The Outcome: Belonging Builds Trust

The result was more than a clearer message. It was a stronger foundation for trust. Bryan's view was that the employer brand is most powerful when it helps people understand how they fit within the organization and that they belong. When that happens, the employer brand becomes something far bigger than recruitment marketing. It becomes a guide for the lived experience of work, helping people understand what they are going to experience, what they are going to get, and what they need to do to succeed. It also offers a direct antidote to the Sunday Scaries. As Bryan put it, those feelings often show up when someone realizes they are in a place where they do not belong, or that the exchange was never made clear in the first place.

While the work created stronger internal clarity and alignment, Bryan was candid that the employer brand did not fully launch externally in the way they had hoped. That experience surfaced one important lesson: marketing and brand partners should have been brought in earlier so the employer brand and consumer brand could sit alongside one another more naturally. That alignment matters because credibility is built when the inside story and outside story both ring true.

Practical Lessons for HR & People Leaders

- Start with Employee Listening. Research the lived experience before you try to write the story.
- Map values to behaviors and then to actions, so people know what the culture actually looks like at work.
- Bring marketing and brand colleagues into the EVP work earlier so the employer brand and consumer brand can align with credibility.

When the inside story matches the outside story, trust grows and the Sunday Scaries start to lose their grip.

The 7-minute reality check (Employer Branding)

Open your careers page. Skim the tagline, your last town hall notes, and your "Our Company Values" poster. Choose one or look at them all. Now grab a pen and be ruthless. Time for an audit. Set a timer for seven minutes and journal through the prompts below:

1. **Where are we overpromising?**

   Circle every word that implies always or never, such as "flexible, high trust, no meetings, or fast growth." Write down the exact moments when that's not true. Name it.

2. **Where do we already have receipts?**

   List the policies, rituals, and metrics that prove a claim. For example: "Flexibility" = core hours 10 a.m.–3 p.m., remote stipend, work-from-home three days, utilization 78%. If it's not a policy, ritual, or number, it's not a receipt.

3. **What confirms or contradicts this in Week One?**

   Imagine a new hire's first five business days on the job.
   What do they see, hear, or do that backs up your promise, or obliterates it? Think: meeting norms, tool access, manager 1:1 meetings, anchor days, and recognition moments.

4. **Are we clear on defaults and exceptions?**

   Write your default, what people can count on, the acceptable exceptions, and who gets to decide. If you can't explain it in two sentences, candidates will assume chaos, as well.

5. **What could we change first to close the biggest gap?**

   Pick one claim. Identify one system change, not a slogan, that you can ship in 30 days. Add an owner and a date.

The takeaway: if you can't point to a policy, ritual, or metric, it's not a promise. It's a wish.

Expectation-setting toolkit (recruiters + hiring managers)

One-liner for the job description:

"We work hybrid: in-office Tuesdays and Thursdays, remote on other days. Core hours are 10 a.m.–3 p.m. for cross-team overlap."

Phone screen script (recruiter):

"Here's how we do flexibility: two anchor days on-site, and we protect core hours from 10 a.m.–3 p.m. Outside that, managers set team norms. Does this fit your reality?"

Hiring manager interview line:

"Autonomy here means clear outcomes and support. You'll own X, with decisions at Y level. When decisions need to escalate, here's how long that typically takes."

Offer letter clause (plain English):

"Our current hybrid policy is Tuesdays and Thursdays on-site, with core hours from 10 a.m.–3 p.m. We review this quarterly and post updates at [link]."

Onboarding slide (Day 1):

> *"Promises we make / Proof you'll see this month:"*
> - **Flex:** Tuesday/Thursday anchor days (calendar norms are live now)
> - **Trust:** "You Said / We Did / Here's What's Next" (last Friday of the month)
> - **Growth:** IDP kickoff in Week 2 (30 minutes with your manager)

Choose-your-own-adventure

- Is your head spinning with too many ideas? Head to page 281.
- Need a pep talk? Head to page 282.
- Need a refresh on employee listening? Head to page 19.
- Want to take action on your talent assessments? Head to the next chapter.

Your employer brand isn't a poster on the office wall. It's pattern recognition:

Say → Do → Show, On Repeat.

When your careers site matches what employees see, feel, and understand at work, you don't need spin. You've got receipts. Be clear in your communication and show your Now → Next promises with owners and dates. Equip your recruiters and hiring managers with the same message map so they avoid overpromising and underdelivering to new hires. Schedule quarterly EVP tune-ups with key stakeholders to make sure the promises your organization makes are actually kept.

Do that long enough and the eye-rolls fade. Offer declines drop. New hires say, "Yep, this is exactly what you told me, and I'm glad I work here."

Next up: move from brand language to talent signals, the clear skills, behaviors, and evidence that help people embody the culture you say you value.

Remember: promises don't build your company. People do.

So, let's turn brand talk into talent signals you hire, grow, and measure. Because culture doesn't come from slogans. It comes from how people show up every day.

Are you ready?

Let's dive in.

It's time to simplify: **Talent Assessments That See the Whole Human.**

TALENT
ASSESSMENTS

3

Talent Assessments That See the Whole Human

"Great talent decisions start by seeing the whole person, not just the résumé, rating, or result."

—Mary

LEARN FROM LAUREN

Potential, not proxies

"No one cares about my career here." Lauren has heard that line three times this week. It stings, because it's not true, but *the system* makes it feel true.

She audits promotions from the last 18 months, and the patterns jump out. The same interview questions. Different standards. Polished resumes over real skills. Vague feedback like "they aren't ready yet."

In a leadership sync, she asks:

Lauren: "What does 'ready' actually mean here?"

VP of Engineering: "You know… presence. Scope. The 'it' factor."

Lauren (deadpan): "Cool, cool. Let's try to measure that 'it' factor."

In round one, she stumbles. She tries a nine-box grid, and managers game it within a day. ("Look, everyone is a HiPo here!")

In round two, she pilots a rubric-based promotion panel with three changes:

- Role outcomes replace fuzzy traits.
- Work samples and simulations replace hypotheticals.
- Evidence packs, built from examples and signals, replace gut feeling.

She also adds internal-move tasks, such as running a real stand-up for a week, shipping a small analysis, or facilitating a cross-team retrospective. The first panel runs in Product and CX. Managers report clearer standards and fewer surprises. Candidates, whether promoted or not, leave with a 90-day growth plan tied to the rubric that feels empowering. The "no one cares" chorus gets noticeably quieter.

Talent Assessments

"If you don't start with a baseline of your skills, how do you know what needs improvement and where to upskill first?"

What it is, simplified.

A whole-human talent assessment is a repeatable way to select, grow, and promote people using evidence of capability, values, and potential, not proxies like pedigree, polish, or proximity.

It aligns:

- **Role outcomes** → what "good" produces
- **Signals** → behaviors you can observe
- **How we measure** → work samples, structured questions, simulations, 360s, and data you can defend

Why it matters now

When promotions feel political, good people disengage or leave.

Structured, evidence-based methods flip that script: higher internal mobility, better diversity through the funnel, and faster time to effectiveness. On the ground, that means fewer surprise denials, tighter calibration, and a clear Now → Next path that keeps high-potentials (HiPos) in the boat longer.

Enter the skills-based workforce.

Stop putting people in buckets based only on title and tenure. Inventory their real skills, including level and proof, map them to business outcomes, and invest to close the gaps. Practically, that means a shared skills taxonomy by role family, team heat maps, and growth signals, like work samples, outcomes, and peer or customer evidence, that travel with the employee, rather than relying only on a manager's opinion.

Promotions and internal moves should hinge on demonstrated capability and clear evidence. Learning paths, micro-assignments, and mentoring should target the exact skills the business needs next.

The payoff is faster team reconfiguration as priorities shift, fairer and more transparent decisions, and a culture where people can see how today's work ladders to tomorrow's role. Skills are the currency, and everyone can earn more of them.

Common mistakes & pitfalls (so you can avoid them)

Most talent mistakes boil down to this: we reward polish, guess at potential, and hope the nine-box will save us.

The fix is simple, not easy: define outcomes, gather clear evidence, and make decisions you can defend in daylight. Use the table below to replace guesswork with structure, fairness, and agility.

Mistake	Solution
Assume résumé proxies mean someone is qualified (school, past titles, or someone having "executive presence").	Define role outcomes and the signals that prove them. Train interviewers to anchor decisions to actual evidence of performance and potential.
Unstructured interviews that reward charisma.	Use a structured question bank with the same questions, scoring guides, and red and green flags. Rotate panelists.
Using the nine-box as a performative tool (labels without development).	Swap it for a Capability × Values rubric, plus a 90-day development plan for each candidate.
Asking hypotheticals only ("What would you do if…?").	Add work samples and simulations. Let people do the real thing at a reduced scope so you can see them in action.
Unclear promotion decisions.	Publish the criteria, run promotion panels, and issue decision memos with growth-focused next steps.
Psychometrics as the sole gatekeeper or source of truth.	If used, treat them as one input, validated for the job, never the sole decision tool. Provide opt-in and a debrief.

One simple tip — #DoTheThing (this week)

Pick one role where people keep disagreeing on who is ready, then name one clear outcome that role should deliver in the next 90 days.

That's it.

Before your next interview, promotion discussion, or internal move conversation, write down:

- **one outcome** this role needs to deliver
- **one signal** that would show the person can do it
- **one way you'll measure it** fairly

For example:

Role: Senior Analyst, CX

Outcome: Deliver weekly insights that influence at least one CX decision each month.

Signal: Turns vague asks into clear questions and a practical analysis plan.

How we'll measure it: Review one real work sample or use a short case exercise with a simple scoring guide.

This small shift helps you stop relying on vibes, charisma, or gut feel. It gives managers and candidates a clearer picture of what "ready" actually means.

Quick tip: Don't try to redesign the whole process this week. Just make one decision more evidence-based than the last one.

Goal: In 30 business days, pilot a whole-human assessment system for one role family, such as Senior IC or Frontline Lead. Publish clear criteria, run structured interviews plus a work sample, hold one promotion or internal-move panel, and deliver 90-day growth plans for those who are ready now and those who are not yet.

Scope: one role family · 2–3 teams · about 8–12 candidates, with a mix of internal moves and promotion candidates

Core artifacts (built during the sprint):

- Role Outcomes → Signals → How We Measure one-pager
- Structured interview kit (questions, scoring rubrics, red and green flags)
- 60–90 minute work sample or simulation plus scoring guide
- Evidence pack template (Outcome → Example → Impact → Corroborating Signal)
- Promotion or selection panel playbook plus decision memo template
- 90-day growth plan template (for promotes and near-misses)
- Change communications: "What's different, why, and what 'ready' means now"

30-day talent assessments sprint

Phase 1 — Focus and draft (Days 1–6)

Day 1: Kickoff (60 minutes). Align on the role family, business outcomes, decision rights, and timeline.

Days 2–3: Draft Role Outcomes (3–5) and Signals (6–10). Pull two recent strong examples to ground the work in reality.

Day 4: Build the structured interview: six questions mapped to outcomes, a 1–4 scoring guide, and red and green flags.

Day 5: Design the work sample, capped at 75 minutes, to mirror real work. Write what good looks like.

Day 6: Create the evidence pack template and decision memo, including why / why not and a 90-day plan.

Optional AI assist: Use AI to draft a first pass of questions and rubrics from your outcomes, then edit for fit and remove bias.

Phase 2 — Calibrate and train (Days 7–10)

Day 7: Panel calibration (60 minutes). Score two historical dossiers using the rubric, then reconcile the gaps.

Day 8: Interviewer training (45–60 minutes). Practice asking questions, taking notes, and scoring to the rubric.

Day 9: Dry-run the work sample with one volunteer, then adjust timing and scoring language.

Day 10: Publish the criteria one-pager to candidates and managers. Follow the "no surprises" rule.

Phase 3 — Run the pilot (Days 11–20)

Days 11–12: Candidate briefings (15 minutes each). Share the process, materials, timelines, and fairness commitments.

Days 13–16: Conduct structured interviews, two per day. Collect scores and short evidence notes the same day.

Days 17–18: Administer work samples. Use two scorers per sample and reconcile within 24 hours.

Day 19: Compile evidence packs, run a quick bias and wording check, and finalize panel packets.

Day 20: Promotion or Internal-Move Panel (90 minutes). Decide, document with decision memos, and assign 90-day plans.

Phase 4 — Communicate and land (Days 21–26)

Days 21–22: Deliver decisions one-on-one to those you aim to promote and the near-misses. Share 90-day growth plans.

Day 23: Manager enablement (30 minutes): how to coach to the rubric, use growth plans, and avoid halo or horn bias.

Day 24: Publish a company-wide process one-pager with the criteria, steps, panel cadence, and appeal path.

Days 25–26: Boost internal mobility: post the next open roles internally for five business days and add a transfer checklist.

Phase 5 — Measure, improve, and scale (Days 27–30)

Day 27: Pull a pilot metrics snapshot: fairness item (Top-2 box), time to decision, evidence-use percentage, and diversity through the funnel.

Day 28: Hold a retrospective (60 minutes). What should you keep, tweak, or drop? Update the interview bank and work sample.

Day 29: Give an executive readout (15 minutes): outcomes, learning, risks, and the next-team rollout plan.

Day 30: Lock the quarterly panel cadence, name owners, and publish the roadmap for the next role family.

Minimal RACI (per role family)

> » **Responsible:** Hiring leader + panelists (apply the rubric, decide, document)
> » **Accountable:** People Ops / Talent (program owner)
> » **Consulted:** Legal / DEI (guardrails), HRBP and Learning & Development team (growth plans)
> » **Informed:** Candidates, managers, ELT

Sprint metrics (track weekly, report at the end of Day 30)

- **Process fairness:** "Criteria were clear" (Top-2 box)
- **Evidence use:** % of decisions with a completed rubric + work sample
- **Time to decision:** candidate briefing → decision memo (median days)
- **Diversity through the funnel:** Apply → Assess → Offer → Accept, internal and external
- **Internal mobility:** number of internal moves in the pilot versus the prior baseline

Risks and fast mitigations

- **Manager drift to gut feel** → Use a two-scorer rule, panel calibration, and decision memos.
- **Work-sample time burden** → Cap it at 75–90 minutes. Protect time

for internal candidates and pay external candidates.

- **Opaque communication** → Publish criteria before interviews and share outcomes with examples afterward.
- **Bias leakage** → Remove identifiers where feasible, run wording and bias checks on notes, and train panelists.

Copy-ready one-liners for communications

- *"We're replacing the guesswork with proof: clear outcomes, structured interviews, and a real work sample."*
- *"No surprises: candidates see the criteria before we assess, and they receive a 90-day development plan either way."*
- *"Panels make the call based on clear evidence. Decisions are grounded in role outcomes, not polish or proximity."*

What scales next (post-pilot)

- Add one more role family per quarter.
- Build a shared work-sample library and question bank.
- Tie promotion readiness to evidence packs, plus a values-based scenario every time.
- Publish a quarterly transparency note with criteria updates, panel dates, and mobility stats.

This sprint gives you visible fairness, faster decisions, and a clear path from Now → Next in 30 business days.

Momentum moves

Capability matrix + heat map

Define what good looks like by role family: Beginner, Proficient, Advanced. Heat map teams and focus development where skills need to be developed and the work needs it most.

Promotion panels, quarterly

Use a cross-functional panel, anonymized evidence packs where feasible, and a standardized decision memo explaining why or why not, plus a 90-day development plan.

Internal moves as the default

Post roles internally for five business days before going external. Publish a transfer checklist to reduce manager friction.

Work-sample library

Build reusable tasks by role. Cap them at 60–90 minutes, score them with rubrics, and offer paid time for external candidates and protected time for internal candidates.

Values in action

Add one values-based scenario to every process and score it like any other outcome.

METRICS THAT MATTER

Track a small set of metrics every month, then review the trend quarterly.

Talent Assessments Metrics	What It Tells You
Internal mobility rate (by org, level, demographic)	Whether your assessment system is actually unlocking within-company moves, and for whom.
Time to effectiveness post-move (days to hit baseline outcomes)	How quickly internal hires reach agreed performance, proof that you selected and supported well.
Process fairness item (Top-2 box on "criteria were clear")	Whether candidates understood the why behind decisions, a core trust signal.
Evidence use (% of decisions with a completed rubric + work sample)	How often choices were grounded in proof instead of vibes.
Regretted attrition among near-misses	Whether strong "not yet" candidates stay, grow, and try again.
Diversity through the funnel (Apply → Assess → Offer → Accept; internal and external)	Where representation drops off, so you can fix the leaks with data instead of guesswork.

Pick three and report on them every month. Consistency beats dashboards that no one opens.

Using AI to simplify (Talent Assessments)

Speed, not judgment. Drafts, not decisions. Always human-owned.

Use Case	Good Prompt	Even Better Prompt
Draft a role outcomes sheet	"Write outcomes for a Senior Data Analyst."	"You are a talent analyst. Draft 4–5 outcomes for a Senior Data Analyst in a B2B SaaS company, tied to decisions influenced and automation delivered. Avoid fluff. Return the outcomes plus 6–8 observable signals. Do not include any personally identifiable information."
Create a structured interview	"Create questions for a Project Manager interview."	"Create six structured questions to assess the outcomes below for a Project Manager role. For each one, include green and red flags plus a 1–4 scoring guide. Keep the language plain. Outcomes: [paste outcomes here]. Return the results as a table."
Design a work sample	"Make a task for a CX Lead."	"Design a 75-minute work sample for a CX Lead. The candidate should analyze 20 tickets, surface three themes, and propose two experiments. Include instructions, materials, a scoring rubric, and what good looks like."
Turn feedback into an evidence pack	"Summarize these notes."	"Convert the notes below into an evidence pack using this structure: Outcome → Example → Impact → Corroborating signal (peer or customer). Remove names. Flag language that may contain bias. Return the result as bullet points."
Bias/wording check	"Check this for bias."	"Review the rubric and interview questions for stereotype risk or coded language. Suggest neutral alternatives. Highlight any criteria that are not tied to outcomes."

Quick AI guardrails reminder:

- Strip names and identifiers before pasting content into AI.
- Do not feed raw candidate data into AI.
- Treat outputs as "dirty first drafts." Humans must stay in the loop and own the final wording and decisions.
- Document where AI assisted for transparency.

REAL-WORLD CASE STUDY

Leadership Assessment, Potential, and the Cost of Getting It Wrong

Employee selection matters at every level of an organization. A single bad front-line hire may seem manageable, but repeated mistakes compound over time, eroding performance and culture. At the executive level, one wrong decision can ripple across teams, disrupt strategy, and create lasting consequences.

Despite this, many organizations still rely on instinct, unstructured interviews, or unsophisticated assessments when making leadership talent decisions.

Brandon Jordan, organizational psychologist and founder of ForPsyte Talent Assessments, sees this pattern repeatedly in his work with leaders and boards evaluating leadership candidates.

The Challenge: High Stakes, Low Rigor

Consider how people approach other major decisions. When buying a car or a home, most would never skip a Carfax report or a professional inspection. Yet organizations routinely make executive hiring decisions with less diligence than a home inspection.

Many believe their intuitions serve them well. But organizational processes and analyses of résumés and interviews are wrought with bias and likely using assessment tools never designed to predict leadership performance.

Organizations struggle to define performance and frequently confuse success in one context with potential in the next.

A strong individual contributor or executive in one setting is often assumed to be high potential everywhere. In practice, leadership (in)effectiveness is highly contextual. What works in one organization, industry, or level may fail in another.

The Peter Principle illustrates this gap. In a meta-analysis of 38,843 sales professionals Benson, Li, and Shue (2018) demonstrated this pattern in sales organizations. Other research shows that current job performance is a weak and inconsistent predictor of later leadership performance (Schleu & Hüffmeier, 2021). High performance at one level does not translate into potential at the next.

The Challenge: You Cannot Test Everything

Research consistently shows that combining multiple assessment methods improves predictive accuracy (Schmidt & Hunter, 1998). However, there are practical limits. Candidates will not tolerate endless testing. Boards and executive teams are highly sensitive to candidate experience.

Recruiting senior leaders is as much about attraction as it is about evaluation.

More data helps, but only to a point. The goal is high quality yet efficient assessment. The right evidence, gathered efficiently, supports stronger decisions economically and creates a good candidate experience.

The Strategy: Assess the Person, the Role, and the Context

Behavior, personality, and cognitive ability are universal constructs. When we say someone is extroverted or intelligent, we agree on what that means.

Asking what it takes to be a successful CFO at a specific company, industry, and culture, requires far more nuance. Leadership (in)effectiveness emerges from how universal traits interact with role demands, culture, and strategy.

Effective leadership assessment begins with a clearly defined success profile or leadership competency model. This forms the foundation for evaluating both performance and potential.

This is where performance and potential diverge. Performance reflects how someone succeeds today. Potential reflects their capacity to succeed in a more complex role tomorrow, often requiring different behaviors and abilities.

Lastly, aligning your assessment tools (personality, cognitive, interviews, judgment, culture, 360) to that defined performance model, whether empirically or conceptually, is the best practice in predicting potential.

The Outcome: Better Decisions and Greater Trust

When used well, leadership assessments improve organizational effectiveness, productivity, and long-term performance. Clearer hiring, promotion, and succession decisions reduce costly derailments and support profitability and retention.

Employees experience decisions as fairer, feedback as more useful, and development conversations as evidence-based rather than subjective. Over time, this consistency strengthens culture and trust, helping organizations build leadership capability with greater confidence.

Practical Lessons for HR and People Leaders

- Define success before you assess it.
- Assess for the next job, not the last one.
- Stop assuming high performance equals high potential.
- Use multiple assessment methods with intention.
- Choose assessment tools using the three C's of validity: Content, Construct, and Criteria.
- Protect the candidate experience.

In the end, better talent assessments do more than improve hiring decisions. They replace guesswork with clarity, bias with evidence, and uncertainty with confidence in the leaders we choose to trust with our organizations.

The 7-minute reality check (Talent Assessments)

Set a timer for seven minutes. Pull up one recent job posting, interview guide, and promotion decision for the same role. Grab a pen. It's time to get it out on paper and gain clarity.

1. **Define outcomes:** For one role, list 3–5 business outcomes this job must deliver in the next 90–180 days.

2. **Name the signals:** For each outcome, write 1–2 observable signals you would actually see or hear on the job that show the person is capable of delivering that outcome.

3. **Retire proxies:** Looking at the last three hiring or promotion decisions for this role, were those decisions based on evidence or on proxies like school, titles, or charisma? Identify one proxy to retire.

4. **Add clear evidence:** Identify one interview, promotion, or internal-move process where you can introduce a 45-minute work sample or simulation this month, and assign a rubric owner.

5. **Make decisions defensible:** Look at a recent "not selected" decision for this role. Could the team clearly point to the criteria and evidence behind it? If not, choose one fix, such as panel calibration, a decision memo, or a standardized interview with a 1–4 scoring guide.

JOT DOWN YOUR IDEAS HERE

FIND BONUS RESOURCES HERE

Choose-your-own-adventure

- Need a brain-break? Head to page 283.
- Want to spark a new idea to get you going on this section? Head to page 284.
- Need a refresh on employee listening? Head to page 19.
- Want to take action on leadership development? Head to the next chapter.

Here's the gut check: if your process still rewards polish over proof, you're gambling with your talent bench. This chapter showed you how to swap vibes for evidence: clear outcomes, structured interviews, real work samples, and decisions you can defend in daylight. Do that, and promotions stop feeling political, internal moves speed up, and your high-potentials can finally see a path forward without leaving.

You now have the tools to run a 30-business-day pilot, publish criteria before you assess, and give every candidate, whether selected or not yet, a fair and specific next step. That's how trust grows: one transparent decision, one shared rubric, one measurable win at a time.

The takeaway: vibes don't build teams. Evidence does.

When you assess for evidence of capability, values, and potential, and show your receipts, careers feel possible, managers decide faster, and your best people stick around to grow. All of this should inform the leadership development plans you build for your high-potential talent and help your workforce feel equipped and empowered to do the best work of their lives.

Are you ready?

Let's dive in.

It's time to simplify: **Leadership Development for a Skills-Based Workforce.**

The Simplifiers Employee Experience Flywheel™

LEADERSHIP
DEVELOPMENT

4

Leadership Development for a Skills-Based Workforce

"A manager can shape someone's entire workday with one conversation, one decision, or one silent moment."

—Mary

From training to traction

"Training request: everything, for everyone, by Friday." That's the email subject line.

Lauren snorts, rolls her eyes at no one in particular, and replies to herself, "Perfect. Right after I invent time travel."

The business unit lead shows up with coffee and good intentions.

Over time, they've built a strong working relationship, and he actually tells her the truth.

"Okay, Allen, give me the three capabilities or skills your team actually needs this quarter," Lauren says, pen poised.

He scans his notes. "Well... I'd say product storytelling, data fluency, and coaching basics."

"Great," she says. "Not 'leadership in general.' Not 'soft skills.' Three. We can do those three."

Fifteen minutes later, a calendar hold hits everyone's inbox: Leadership Lunch-n-Lecture (Mandatory/Optional).

Lauren facepalms.

"Who sent this? Guys, we're not doing a TED Talk with sandwiches."

She messages the organizer directly: "Let's trade the lecture for practice labs. Also, no stale pizza bribes. And just curious... how can something be both 'optional' and 'mandatory' at the same time?"

She tours the LMS training catalog. Yep, there are 87 courses, most built in the 2010s, and one titled *Excel for Winners* that was last updated when flip phones were still hot.

Cue another eye roll. "Holy moly. We're building learning paths, not a museum."

In the manager roundtable, someone asks, "Can we get a 12-minute training on coaching?"

Resisting the urge to clap back, Lauren catches herself and regains her composure.

"Great idea, but I think people tune out if it's all just theory. How about a 30-minute practice lab where you actually try it," Lauren says. "With a rubric. And a timer."

Silence. Then a cautious nod. "Okay... if there's a timer."

From there, she ships three things fast:

- a one-page Individual Development Plan (IDP) that employees own, not a 14-tab, overly complicated spreadsheet
- a lightweight capability matrix for each function showing what good looks like right now
- monthly peer-run practice labs built around Watch → Try → Ship,

where people run short drills on real work to build skills in a low-risk environment

Slack lights up: "Do I get credit if I watch the practice lab at 2x speed?"

She chuckles. "Only if your customer can hear you speak at 2x," Lauren replies.

Finance asks for ROI before week one. IT asks her to "open a ticket to request permission to open a ticket."

She breathes, cracks a smile, and keeps it simple: "We'll measure shipped outputs and time to effectiveness. Give me 30 business days."

Within a quarter, stretch goals are clearer, managers are sponsoring bite-size micro-assignments, and the infamous "Mandatory/Optional" holds quietly disappear. Voluntary attrition in the pilot teams ticks down too.

A supervisor emails: "My new analyst used the data storytelling playbook, and we landed a decision in one meeting. Also… thank you for 86-ing the Lunch-n-Lecture. I'm loving what you're doing. It's way, way better."

Leadership Development

"Your edge isn't headcount. It's skill depth at every layer. Build a plan that develops Individual Contributors (ICs), People Leaders, and the Executive Leadership Team (ELT) in lockstep with your Now → Next strategy."

What it is, simplified.

The social contract at work has changed. People won't trade their Mondays for vague promises anymore. They expect real investment in their growth, whether they stay two years or ten.

Leadership development is a core clause in that new deal, not a perk for the chosen few.

Done right, the employee drives the Individual Development Plan (IDP) and takes ownership on completing it, choosing two or three capabilities that ladder up to business outcomes. The manager's job is to clear roadblocks, offer coaching and accountability, and create space to practice in the flow of work. HR's job is to make the system simple and fair through:

- a one-page IDP
- a shared skills language
- practice labs built on real scenarios
- access rules that keep opportunities from going to the usual suspects

When the tools are simple and easy to use, the rhythm of leadership development becomes predictable. It stops being something we only do when we're "not in launch mode" or "not in busy season." *Spoiler alert: we're always in busy season these days.*

The result? Managers actually use, and champion, the tools. Employees see progress they can point to: new skills, shipped work, and visible receipts. Just as important, they feel empowered too, like the company actually cares about their professional development. That goes a long way.

And that's how trust grows. Not from slogans, but from repetition that builds confidence, respect, and career momentum. This is a paradigm shift: even if an employee eventually takes those skills elsewhere, your culture still wins, now and later, because people who feel invested in will do better work today and speak well of you tomorrow.

Why it matters now

Budgets are flat, priorities keep zig-zagging, and your skill gaps aren't going to wait for a quarterly offsite.

Teams that build capability in the flow of work ramp faster, retain more high-potential employees (HiPos), and move talent where the business needs it most without crushing morale.

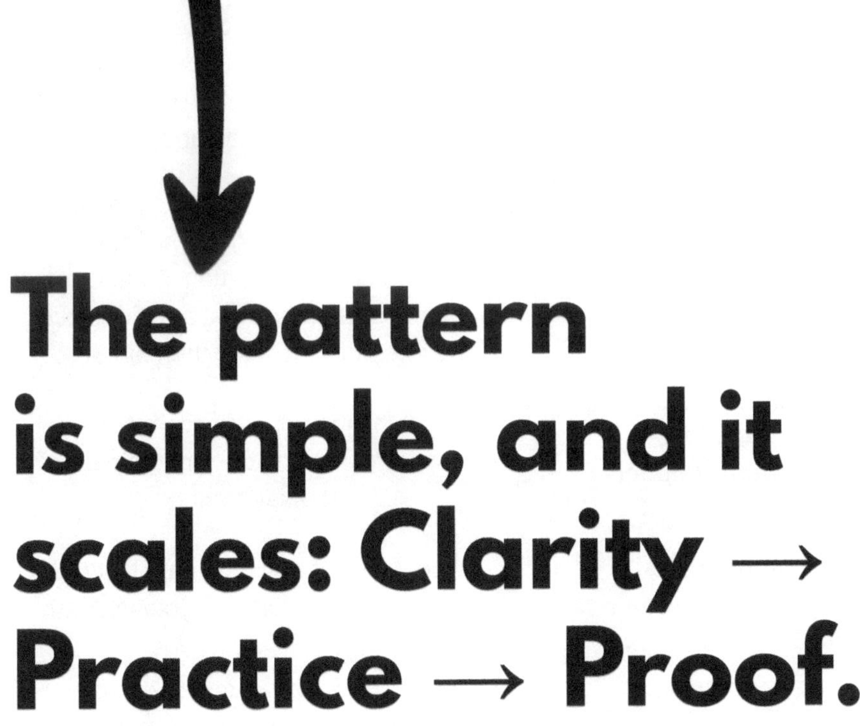

The pattern is simple, and it scales: Clarity → Practice → Proof.

Skills are the currency.
Invest in your people every day, and you'll see the returns compound.

Common mistakes & pitfalls (so you can avoid them)

Mistake	Solution
Spray-and-pray training (big catalogs, low usage)	Build paths, not piles: Watch → Try → Ship on real deliverables.
Manager buy-in is assumed	Give managers a 10-minute coaching kit for each path. Make "remove roadblocks" part of their role and teach them how to do so.
IDPs become paperwork or busy work	Keep the IDP to one page, tied to role outcomes, next capabilities, and a 90-day practice plan. Make it employee-owned and driven.
No time to practice, so they rush through the training	Create monthly 45-minute practice labs with high reps, real scenarios, and peer facilitation. Focus on micro-learnings that are bite-sized and interactive to keep them engaged.
Access favors the usual suspects	Publish open calls for micro-assignments and track participation by segment.
No receipts, so you can't show impact	Track outputs shipped, capability lift, and internal mobility tied to each path.
AI writes the plan	Let AI draft, but humans decide. Strip personally identifiable information (PII), check for bias, and keep the context local.

One simple tip — #DoTheThing (this week)

Pick one role. In 60 minutes, create a one-page IDP template, draft a starter learning path with no more than three items, and announce a 30-minute practice lab for next week. Flip ahead to see how AI can help you brainstorm a first draft.

Remember: small, visible, and real beats perfect.

IDP (copy/paste):

Role:

Role outcomes (create 3–4):

1.
2.
3.
4.

Next capability or skill to build (choose 1–2):

1.
2.

90-day practice plan (what will they work on to build this skill?):

Micro-assignment:

Practice lab date:

Mentor or peer partner:

Success signal (how we'll know the skill is developing):

30-day leadership development sprint

Goal: In 30 business days, launch a simple leadership development system for one team or role group: publish a one-page IDP, define the top capabilities to build, run one practice lab, assign one micro-assignment, and equip managers to coach progress in the flow of work.

Scope: one team or role group | 1–2 target capabilities | 8–15 employees max for the pilot

Core artifacts (built during the sprint):

- One-page Individual Development Plan (IDP)
- Capability matrix for the pilot group
- Starter learning path (Watch → Try → Ship)
- One 45-minute practice lab
- One micro-assignment tied to real work
- Manager coaching guide for 1:1s
- Simple metrics tracker
- Communication note: what's changing, why, and how this helps people grow

Phase 1 — Focus and define (Days 1–6)

Day 1: Kickoff (45–60 minutes). Choose the pilot group, clarify business priorities, and identify the one or two capabilities that matter most right now.

Day 2: Define what good looks like. Write simple descriptions of the target capabilities and the behaviors that show progress.

Day 3: Build the one-page IDP template. Keep it focused on role outcomes, next capability, 90-day practice plan, and success signal.

Day 4: Draft a starter learning path with no more than three items: one thing to watch, one thing to try, and one thing to ship.

Day 5: Design one micro-assignment tied to real work, with a named sponsor and clear success criteria.

Day 6: Create the manager coaching guide with 1:1 prompts, common roadblocks, and signals to watch for.

Optional AI assist: Use AI to draft the first pass of the capability matrix, practice lab outline, or IDP template, then edit for fit, tone, and bias.

Phase 2 — Build and align (Days 7–10)

Day 7: Review the pilot with managers. Align on expectations, timelines, and what support employees will need.

Day 8: Finalize the capability matrix and starter learning path.

Day 9: Build the 45-minute practice lab using a real scenario from current work.

Day 10: Publish the pilot materials: IDP template, learning path, practice lab date, and manager guide.

Phase 3 — Launch the pilot (Days 11–20)

Days 11–12: Introduce the pilot to employees. Explain what's changing, why it matters, and what they can expect.

Days 13–14: Employees complete the one-page IDP with manager input.

Days 15–16: Managers hold short 1:1s to confirm the next capability, the micro-assignment, and the success signal.

Day 17: Run the first practice lab. Keep it practical, peer-based, and tied to real work.

Days 18–20: Launch the micro-assignments and confirm sponsor support, calendar time, and expected outcomes.

Phase 4 — Coach and reinforce (Days 21–26)

Day 21: Managers use the coaching guide in 1:1s to check progress, remove roadblocks, and reinforce effort.

Day 22: Gather quick feedback from employees and managers on what feels clear, useful, and too heavy.

Day 23: Adjust the practice lab, learning path, or IDP based on early feedback.

Day 24: Share one visible example of progress from the pilot, such as a shipped output, a new behavior, or a manager success story.

Days 25–26: Run a second round of coaching check-ins and collect a few proof points.

Phase 5 — Measure, improve, and extend (Days 27–30)

Day 27: Pull a simple pilot snapshot: IDP completion, lab participation, micro-assignment progress, and one manager behavior metric.

Day 28: Hold a short retrospective. What should you keep, simplify, or improve?

Day 29: Share a one-slide readout with senior leaders: what you launched, what's working, and what comes next.

Day 30: Name owners, lock the next practice lab date, and decide whether to extend the pilot to another team or capability.

Minimal RACI (for the pilot)

> » **Responsible:** Managers and employees (complete IDPs, practice, apply learning)
> » **Accountable:** People Ops / L&D (pilot owner)
> » **Consulted:** Business leader, HRBP, functional subject matter experts
> » **Informed:** Pilot participants, senior leaders, future managers of the next rollout group

Sprint metrics (track weekly, report at the end of Day 30)

- IDP completion rate: % of pilot participants with a completed one-page IDP
- Practice lab participation: % of employees who attended and participated
- Micro-assignment completion: % of employees who started or completed the assignment
- Manager coaching behavior: % of 1:1s completed with growth discussion included
- Capability confidence: quick pre/post pulse from employees

and managers on the target skill

- Visible proof: number of shipped outputs, practice reps completed, or role-relevant examples collected

Risks and fast mitigations

- Too much content at once → Limit the pilot to one or two skills or capabilities and no more than three learning items.
- Managers don't coach consistently → Give them a short guide, five prompts, and one weekly expectation.
- Practice stays theoretical → Tie the practice lab and micro-assignment to real work already happening.
- Employees see it as extra work → Protect calendar time and make the assignment useful to real business goals.
- No proof of progress → Define one simple success signal upfront and collect examples as you go.

Copy-ready one-liners for communications

- *"We're making development easier to use and easier to prove."*
- *"This pilot is built around real work, not extra busy work."*
- *"Every employee in the pilot will leave with a clear next skill, one practice plan, and one visible way to show progress."*
- *"Managers are not here to own the plan for employees. They are here to coach, support, run alongside, and remove roadblocks."*

What scales next (post-pilot)

- add one more team or role group next quarter
- build a reusable practice lab library
- standardize the one-page IDP across teams
- publish a simple capability matrix for each role group
- track participation and visible proof quarterly
- create a shared manager coaching toolkit for every path

This sprint helps you move leadership development out of theory and into motion, with tools people will actually use and proof leaders can actually see.

Momentum moves (build momentum that lasts)

Capability matrix + heat map: Define what good looks like for each role family by outlining outcomes and behaviors, then visualize current versus target levels by team. Use the color-coded gaps to guide budget, coaching time, and micro-assignment slots, not gut feel.

Practice lab calendar: Schedule monthly, peer-run, 45-minute practice labs built around real scenarios from the last sprint. Rotate a facilitator and a note-taker, keep tight time boxes, and end with a two-minute commitment on what each person will try that week.

Micro-assignments (2–6 weeks): Offer scoped stretch work tied to actual deliverables, with clear success criteria, a named sponsor, and protected calendar time. Close with a quick debrief on what worked, what didn't, and what was learned. Ask: What do I know now that I didn't know before this project? That's how the learning becomes clear evidence.

Mentoring, on purpose: Match mentors and mentees based on the next skill or capability to build, not convenience. Use a simple Mentoring Map: Story → Lesson → Application, so every session ends with one concrete action the mentee will try before the next meeting.

Manager enablement: Give leaders a 10-minute brief for each learning path, including goals, signals to watch for, and common traps. Add five ready-to-use coaching prompts for 1:1s and a "remove roadblocks" checklist covering people, tools, and priority swaps they can act on within a week.

Quarterly talent flight check: Refresh each employee's IDP, review progress on learning paths, and choose one next skill or capability with a matching micro-assignment. Capture it in the system, assign an owner, and set a date to review the evidence together.

METRICS THAT MATTER

Leadership Development Metrics	What It Tells You
IDP adoption and completion (by org/segment)	Whether employees are actually using the growth plan, and where uptake is lagging.
Path participation → outputs shipped	Whether learning is turning into real, shippable work.
Capability lift (pre/post self-assessment + manager signals)	Whether the target skill is actually growing, not just course completions.
Internal mobility (moves within 6–12 months post-path)	Whether development pathways are creating real career movement.
Pilot attrition (voluntary delta versus baseline)	Whether focused development is reducing regretted exits in pilot groups.
Manager behaviors (1:1 cadence, roadblocks cleared, recognition tied to growth)	Whether managers are doing the habits that make development stick.

Pick three to publish monthly. Consistency beats complexity.

Using AI to simplify (Leadership Development)

Use Case	Good Prompt	Even Better Prompt
Draft a capability matrix	"Create a capability matrix for Product Marketing."	"You are an L&D partner with 10+ years of experience. Draft a capability matrix for Product Marketing with four levels, from Associate to Senior Director, across these capabilities: product storytelling, data fluency, stakeholder influence, and coaching basics. For each cell, include behavioral indicators and examples of evidence tied to real deliverables. Return the output as a markdown table."
Build a learning path	"Create a learning path for data fluency."	"Design a Watch → Try → Ship learning path for 'data fluency for PMs' using no more than three resources. Include one practice lab scenario and one micro-assignment that ships value in four hours or less. Return the output as a checklist employees can copy and use."
Write a practice lab	"Create a practice lab."	"Create a 45-minute practice lab on product storytelling. Include an agenda with time boxes, a realistic prompt, a 1–4 scoring rubric, and a three-question debrief. Tone: practical and peer-run. Return the output in markdown."
IDP starter kit	"Write an IDP."	"Generate a one-page IDP template tied to role outcomes and next capabilities. Include a 90-day practice plan section with a micro-assignment, mentor, and success signal. Keep the language plain English and easy to implement. Also create a standard agenda for check-in meetings with a people leader or manager."
Bias and privacy check	"Check this for issues."	"Act as a privacy and bias checker. 1) Flag any personally identifiable information (PII) or sensitive data and suggest anonymization. 2) Identify biased phrasing and offer neutral alternatives. 3) Note any over-promises. Return the output as a three-part checklist."

Quick AI guardrails reminder:

- Strip names and any personally identifiable information (PII) before pasting content into AI. This includes company trade secrets as well.
- Treat outputs as "dirty first drafts." A human should always review, proofread, and own the final wording and decisions.
- Review every output for bias, hallucinations, and errors.
- Log what AI touched for transparency.

REAL-WORLD CASE STUDY

Building "Ready-Now" Leaders in a Global Matrix

Most leadership gaps surface at moments of transition, not in steady state. A senior leader leaves. A critical role opens unexpectedly. And suddenly, there is no one ready to step in.

Like many organizations, **the Head of Talent Development at a large, highly matrixed global enterprise** was facing this exact situation. Responsible for the U.S. workforce of roughly 4,500 employees across enterprise onboarding, functional skill development, leadership development, and executive programs, this leader had a front-row view into how performance pressure, time scarcity, and organizational complexity weakened succession readiness. The result was not only a lack of "ready now" talent, but a system that made building a pipeline of leaders difficult.

The Challenge: A Thin Succession Bench in a Pressure-Cooker Culture

For many leaders in the business, the challenge was building a pipeline of next-level leaders within an overly demanding, deeply matrixed, performance-driven culture while still sustaining business results and employee engagement.

Talent reviews happened annually across most teams, although some leaders reviewed talent more frequently. Many leaders partnered with HR and Talent Development to identify stretch assignments or development opportunities for their high-potential employees, while others needed more support navigating how to do that consistently. Because business performance remained the top priority, leaders were thoughtful about nominating employees for development programs and confirming they could support the time commitment. In some cases, leaders chose to delay participation with a future cohort, only when business conditions allowed for greater focus on development.

Accountability for development was also complex because of the global, matrixed environment. Was responsibility held by senior leadership, HR, Talent Development, or the global L&D teams? Because of the ambiguity, getting alignment on the goal and the focus of the program was critically important.

The Strategy: Build a Strategic Program Focused on Enhancing Readiness

To begin addressing the issue, the Talent Development team focused on high potential Director+ employees who were nominated jointly by their leadership team and HR to participate in the program. Leaders agreed to the time commitment required before placing someone into the program to ensure participants could fully engage.

Program content was informed in part by data already available, including leadership assessments, employee feedback, sentiment data, and executive interviews. These insights revealed consistent capability gaps and informed a six-month, cohort-based program focused on emotional intelligence, leading with empathy, cross-functional influence, coaching skills, and navigating a complex global matrix.

Participants completed emotional intelligence assessments, worked with individual coaches, and intentionally built cross-functional relationships beyond their day-to-day roles. This expanded their understanding of how the broader business operated and strengthened internal networks critical for future leadership roles. Participants also engaged in candid conversations with senior leaders about the realities of VP-level roles, including scope, trade-offs, and pressure. Cohorts were intentionally small to deepen trust and connection across functions.

Development was intentionally experiential and designed to fit within the flow of work rather than compete with it. The ultimate goal was to increase capabilities and readiness so participants could effectively step into next-level roles when opportunities became available.

The Outcome: Stronger Confidence, Clearer Readiness, Better Transitions

Participants reported increased self-awareness, deeper business understanding, stronger internal networks, and greater confidence navigating the organization's matrix. More importantly, those who were promoted appeared better prepared emotionally, relationally, and strategically for their new role compared to those who did not complete the program. As a result, they were able to make meaningful contributions much sooner.

Practical Lessons for HR & People Leaders

- Intentionally build readiness into your programs. Identification without development creates risk.
- Start with the data you already have. Assessments, feedback, and leader insight reveal real gaps.
- Make development part of real work. Relationships, influence, and decision-making matter more than courses.

Leadership pipelines do not fail because people lack ambition. They fail when development is treated as optional. Here, we see what's possible when readiness is built deliberately, within the realities of day-to-day work.

The 7-minute reality check
(Leadership Development)

Set a timer for seven minutes. Open three things: your latest IDP template, LMS completions report, and a manager 1:1 agenda. Grab a pen. Clarity beats wishful thinking.

1. **Define the lift:** For one team, list the top one or two capabilities that need to improve in the next 90 days.

2. **Turn training into outcomes:** For each capability, write one on-the-job result you would expect to see if the learning is working.

3. **Design one rep, not a full program:** Jot down one 45-minute practice lab you could run this month and name the facilitator.

4. **Choose one micro-assignment:** Pick one stretch task tied to one capability. Write the success criteria in a single sentence and name the sponsor.

5. **Make it equitable:** Note one way access is currently offered and one thing you could change to avoid relying on the usual suspects.

6. **Managers as multipliers:** Circle one manager habit you want reinforced weekly and note how you'll remind or track it.

7. **Measure what matters:** Choose one lead metric and one lag metric you would track to know whether this is working.

8. **Before you finish:** Pick one item to #DoTheThing this week, and put it on your calendar before you move on.

JOT DOWN YOUR IDEAS HERE

FIND BONUS RESOURCES HERE

Choose-your-own-adventure

- On the verge of a teeny-tiny menty B? Head to page 285.
- Need a spark of positive inspiration? Head to page 286.
- Need a refresh on employee listening? Head to page 19.
- Want to take action on succession planning? Head to the next chapter.

You've built the leadership development machine: clear outcomes, honest IDPs, practice that sticks, and proof you can show. Next up is making sure the right people are ready for the right roles *before* you need them, without guessing or politics. Bench strength beats backfill every time. Train for the role before it opens.

Yup, we're talking about succession planning! And if your organization doesn't have a plan yet, no worries. Everyone starts somewhere. I'll show you how to make one.

Are you ready?

Let's dive in.

It's time to simplify: **Succession Planning: Making a Plan for Now vs. Next.**

The Simplifiers Employee Experience Flywheel™

SUCCESSION PLANNING

5

Succession Planning: Making a Plan for Now vs. Next

"The future of your culture depends on who is ready to lead next."

—Mary

From opinions to proof

"Great news," the COO says. "We dusted off the nine-box."

Lauren smiles. "Cool. Does it tell us who can run the Q2 launch if Priya gets poached next week?"

Silence. Coffee hasn't kicked in yet.

Armed with real signals from talent assessments and momentum from the new leadership development program overhaul, she shifts succession planning from opinions to proof.

First move: a fast role-risk map. Which roles stall revenue or safety if they suddenly go dark?

Then she defines readiness in plain English:

- Ready now
- Ready soon in 6–12 months
- Ready later in 12+ months

…each one tied to observable evidence of capability, not just job titles.

Next, she posts three scoped stretch projects on the internal marketplace to surface hidden talent:

- Run a cross-team launch retrospective.
- Stand up a customer-feedback loop.
- Own the Ops KPI dashboard.

Two frontline supervisors raise their hands, deliver clear artifacts, things like docs, dashboards, and decisions, and enter the bench with receipts. A director who has been passed over for promotions year after year finally moves to ready soon after being assigned a 90-day capability sprint. She wires it all into the HRIS, remembering that bench status should move with delivered work, not tee times.

By the next quarterly review, the conversation isn't a vibe session. It's a scoreboard: roles, risk, readiness, next actions.

Scenario plans beat tap-on-the-shoulder bias every single time. Internal mobility moves faster. Backfills happen faster. Surprises shrink. Trust grows. This is succession planning for Now vs. Next: dynamic, inclusive, and powered by proof.

Standing confident in her work, she knows: this is the way.

Succession Planning

"Who sits at the core of what makes your organization run smoothly? What skills do they possess? And who are you coaching, mentoring, and preparing to take their place one day, when they get promoted or lured away?"

What it is, simplified.

Succession planning is a living system that ensures your most critical work always has ready humans, now and next.

Prepare for the curveballs of corporate life by:

- mapping role risk: what breaks if this role goes dark or someone goes on parental leave?
- defining "ready" in plain English with outcomes and evidence
- running short development sprints to close skill gaps

Stretch assignments, visible evidence of readiness, and panel reviews replace tap-on-the-shoulder guesswork.

The result is not a dusty spreadsheet that is outdated the second you publish it. It's an active bench that updates when real work ships. When someone moves or leaves, you don't panic. You promote with proof, using live data to inform the call.

Why it matters now

When a pivotal role, one that drives revenue, safety, or key decision-making, sits open, the cost isn't just salary. It can jeopardize critical launches, stall projects, and drive people out. Teams with dynamic benches, with identified ready now and ready soon backups, bounce back faster after exits, keep customer promises, and retain high-potential employees (HiPos) who can see a future without leaving.

The pattern is simple: know which roles matter, define readiness in observable terms, and create proof on purpose.

Common mistakes & pitfalls (so you can avoid them)

Mistake	Solution
Static nine-box labels with no actions	Replace them with Role Risk × Readiness boards and name one gap-closing sprint per person.
Tap-on-the-shoulder bias	Open stretch work through a talent marketplace. Require posted criteria and debriefs.
Readiness = charisma + tenure	Define readiness by outcomes and signals. Use work samples and evidence packs.
Plans built in silos	Run a cross-functional bench review quarterly with Finance, Operations, Product, and People at the same table.
No backfill for managers who develop people, so they hoard talent	Add a manager mobility metric and give temporary headcount cover when leaders graduate talent.
Secret plans, where no one knows the path	Publish role profiles with ready-soon capabilities and the Now → Next actions to get there.
Panic hiring	Maintain a Critical Role Roster with two names per role and a 30/60/90-day coverage plan.

One simple tip — #DoTheThing (this week)

Pick one mission-critical role in your organization.

In 60 minutes, draft:

- Role Outcomes (choose 3–5) → Readiness Signals (define 6–8) → Evidence to Prove It (work sample and artifacts)
- Then post one 4–6 week stretch assignment tied to those signals.
- Name the reviewer. Done.

Definitions (so you can act fast)

Role Outcomes (choose 3–5): The business results this role must deliver in the next 90–180 days, stated as outcomes, not tasks.

Example: "Ship an on-time Q2 release that meets Service Level Agreement (SLA) and Net Promoter Score (NPS) targets."

Readiness Signals (define 6–8): Observable behaviors or skills that predict those outcomes, things you can see and hear in real work.

Example: "Turns ambiguous asks into a scoped plan with risks, owners, and dates."

Evidence to Prove It: The concrete artifacts or simulations that show those signals are real. This is what good looks like.

Example: a 60-minute work sample plus a submitted requirements document, dashboard, or decision memo, scored against a 1–4 rubric that defines what good looks like.

30-day succession planning sprint

Days 1–3: Map the risk

List the top 10 pivotal roles by business impact. Score risk as Impact × Vacancy Likelihood.

Pick three roles for this sprint. Align on owners.

Days 4–6: Define readiness

For each role, write outcomes, signals, work samples, and what good looks like.

Publish a one-pager internally. No surprises.

Days 7–10: Open stretch work

Post 2–3 assignments per role on your internal marketplace, or a simple form.

Require manager approval for the time box, and name scorers and dates.

Days 11–18: Run and review

Candidates do the work, scoped tightly. Two scorers complete rubrics within 24 hours.

Build a short evidence pack per candidate with outputs, feedback, and self-reflection.

Days 19–22: Bench the talent

The panel meets for 60 minutes and places names into Ready Now, Ready Soon, or Build for each role.

Assign one gap-closing sprint, 30–60 days, for each Ready Soon candidate.

Days 23–26: Communicate and cover

Tell each person privately: decision, next steps, and sponsor.

Publish an anonymized bench heat map and the next posting date.

Days 27–30: Lock the cadence

Add bench review to the quarterly calendar.

Give recommendations for upskilling bench talent so the work can be integrated into their existing IDP this quarter.

Update the Critical Role Roster with coverage plans and owners.

Momentum moves

Talent marketplace (lightweight): A simple posted board for stretch assignments with criteria, time commitment, and reviewers. Rotate across functions so hidden talent surfaces.

Ready Soon sprints: 6–8 week, scope-realistic projects with a mentor and a clear exit-to-ready checklist.

Cross-train cadences: Pair roles with overlapping responsibilities. Run shadow weeks and reversible delegations.

Manager mobility goal: Track and recognize leaders who graduate people across teams. Give them temporary backfill credit.

Emergency drills: Twice a year, simulate a sudden vacancy in a critical role. Who covers week 1, week 4, and week 12? Fix the gaps you find.

Teach your people leaders and managers how to run this exercise with their own teams.

METRICS THAT MATTER

Succession Planning Metrics	What It Tells You
Coverage (% of pivotal roles with two or more named successors: Ready Now / Ready Soon)	Bench depth for your most critical roles and how exposed you are if someone leaves.
Time to effectiveness (days to reach agreed outcomes in role)	How quickly successors hit the outcomes you defined, your readiness signal in action.
Internal mobility rate (lateral + upward moves into critical roles, by function and identity group)	Whether opportunities are real and equitably distributed across teams and demographics.
Bench movement (number progressed from Build → Ready Soon → Ready Now per quarter)	Pipeline health and whether development sprints are creating upward motion.
Stretch participation and completion (posted vs. filled vs. completed, with ratings)	Whether your talent marketplace is working and producing quality evidence.
Regretted attrition of HiPos (trend pre- and post-sprint)	Whether stronger paths and fairer decisions are helping you keep your best people.

Pick three to four metrics you'll publish every quarter.

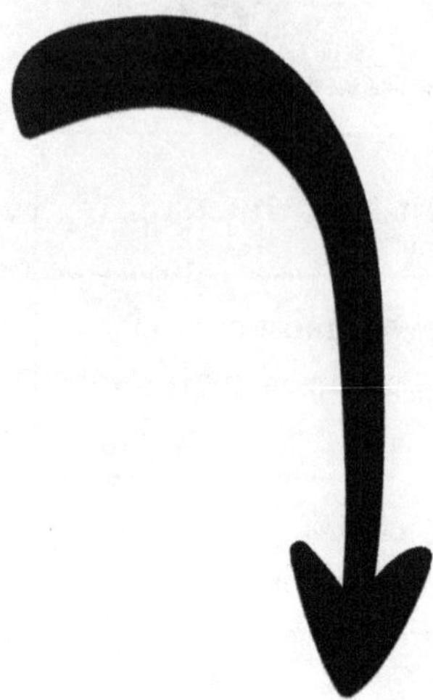

Consistency beats complexity.

Using AI to simplify (Succession Planning)

Use Case	Good Prompt	Even Better Prompt
Role-risk draft	"Rank our roles by risk."	"Act as a People Ops analyst. Given these roles and impacts, propose a Risk = Impact × Likelihood score and rank the top 10. Return a table with role, impact rationale (12 words or fewer), likelihood rationale (12 words or fewer), overall risk score, and a one-line mitigation."
Readiness builder	"Write readiness criteria for this role."	"From these role outcomes, draft 6–8 observable readiness signals and a 60-minute work sample with a 1–4 rubric and 'what good looks like.' Keep the language plain and job-specific. Return a one-pager managers can share with candidates."
Stretch posting generator	"Make a stretch assignment."	"Create three scoped stretch assignments that prove signals A, B, and C. For each, include: time box (2–6 weeks), required artifacts, reviewers (two names or roles), and pass/fail criteria. Then write the posting text employees will see."
Evidence-pack formatter	"Summarize this candidate."	"Summarize this candidate's artifacts into a one-page evidence pack: outcomes delivered, concrete examples (links or file names), peer or customer signals, and de-biased notes tied to the rubric. End with a decision snapshot: Ready Now / 6–12 months / 18+ months, plus why."
Bias and privacy checker	"Check this for issues."	"Act as a privacy and bias checker for the bench summary below. 1) Highlight any personally identifiable information (PII) or sensitive data and suggest anonymization. 2) Flag biased language and offer neutral rewrites. 3) Note any over-promises or vague timelines and propose precise alternatives. Return a three-part checklist."

Quick AI guardrails reminder:

- Strip names, employee identifiers, and any personally identifiable information (PII) before pasting anything into AI. This also includes confidential company information and trade secrets.
- Treat every output as a "dirty first draft." A human should always review, proofread, and own the final wording, recommendations, and decisions.
- Use AI to organize and sharpen the thinking, not to make succession decisions for you. Always review for bias, hallucinations, and factual errors.
- Log what AI touched for transparency, especially when it influences readiness criteria, bench summaries, or internal talent recommendations.

REAL-WORLD CASE STUDY

Succession Planning That Stops Guessing

Growth has a way of exposing what an organization has not planned for yet: leadership continuity.

Theresa Carik, Ph.D., VP, Principal Consultant at Right Management, saw this in a technical consulting firm facing an executive retirement. What looked like one replacement decision quickly became a bigger question about the leadership the business would need next.

The Challenge: Succession Built on Assumptions

The firm's President was preparing to retire. He also served as Head of Office at headquarters, so the organization had to decide whether to replace one person in a dual role or split the job into two positions.

The larger issue was that the company had no formal succession process.

Decisions were shaped by familiarity, assumptions, and visibility. In a technical environment with remote offices, leaders did not always have a clear view of who had the actual strengths, interest, or readiness to step up.

One person at headquarters was widely assumed to want the role, even though no one had *actually* asked him. Leaders were unsure if he was the best fit, but also worried that if they passed him over, he might leave. Theresa saw the company relying too heavily on assumptions instead of real data.

In technical organizations, strong subject matter experts do not always translate into great leadership at the top.

The Strategy: Radical Transparency, Backed by Data

Theresa first helped leaders define what the future required. As they looked at the company's growth plans, it became clear the business likely needed two roles, not one, and that each role required a different mix of strengths.

Then came the part that mattered most for this audience: making the process easy to understand. This leadership team was highly analytical, and succession planning felt foreign. Theresa walked them through the process step by step, explained what each phase was measuring, shared timelines, invited questions, and followed up in writing. Her goal was simple: no confusion and no surprises.

With that foundation in place, she built a structured assessment process using cognitive and personality assessments, interviews, and role plays. It gave candidates a fair chance to show how they think, lead, and respond in real business situations. She then translated the results into a simple talent grid (color-coded: green, yellow, red) so leaders could quickly see who was ready now, who could be ready next, and where development was needed.

The Outcome: Internal Mobility Builds Trust

In the end, the company filled both roles internally, and the transition was seamless.

The process also surfaced overlooked talent, including a leader in a remote office who had much stronger people leadership skills than they realized. It also confirmed that the presumed frontrunner did not want the top role, helping the company avoid a costly mismatch.

Just as important, the work extended beyond the top roles. Filling the roles internally sent a clear signal to employees that there was real opportunity to grow here. Theresa noted that when there is zero internal mobility, that is why people leave.

She also stressed the domino effect. Once two leaders moved up, the company had to plan for the roles they left behind. That led the organization to assess the next layer and start development planning. Employees were hungry for feedback, and the process helped meet that need while building a stronger bench for the future.

Practical Lessons for HR & People Leaders

- Define the future role first. If the business is changing, the role may need to change too.
- Replace assumptions with data. Assessments, interviews, and role plays surface talent that visibility alone misses.
- Build beyond the top seat. Succession planning works best when it strengthens the next layer of leaders too.

This is how organizations turn leadership transitions into growth opportunities.

The 7-minute reality check
(Succession Planning)

Set a timer for seven minutes. No polishing or overthinking, just time to put the truth on paper.

1. **Which three roles, if vacant, would stall revenue or risk customer retention next month? Why?**
2. **Write one readiness signal you would need to see for each of those roles.**
3. **Where are we still doing tap-on-the-shoulder placement? Name one possible fix.**
4. **What stretch assignment could we post next Monday to surface hidden talent?**
5. **Who owns the bench review, and when is it on the calendar?**

**JOT DOWN
YOUR IDEAS
HERE**

**FIND
BONUS
RESOURCES
HERE**

Choose-your-own-adventure

- Need a quick brain break? Head to page 285.
- Need to get centered and regulate your nervous system? Head to page 288.
- Need a refresh on employee listening? Head to page 19.
- Want to take action on your recognition & engagement programs? Head to the next chapter.

You've built a living bench: roles defined by outcomes, readiness you can prove, and opportunity paths that are clear. That's how you keep momentum when promotions, parental leave, or poaching knock on your door. Your employees will appreciate the clarity around what it takes to move inside your organization. They'll start to imagine a career path, take charge of their Individual Development Plan (IDP), and feel empowered to raise their hands for stretch assignments.

Remember, you hired adults. Treat them like one.

When you show people how succession works in your organization, trust and respect grow. No surprises. No popularity contests. Just clear priorities and leaders who guide people along the way.

Next, we'll zoom out to the Recognition + Engagement engine that keeps people energized between the big moves, because careers are marathons, not just finish-line photos.

Are you ready?

Let's dive in.

It's time to simplify: **Recognition + Engagement: From Performative to Powerful.**

The Simplifiers Employee Experience Flywheel™

RECOGNITION +
ENGAGEMENT

6

Recognition + Engagement: From Performative to Powerful

"When effort is expected but appreciation is rare, energy starts to fade."

—Mary

No more mashed potato bars

Tasked with the annual awards and holiday party, Lauren opens last year's deck and groans. "Same stage. Same speeches. Same swag." She shuts the laptop and rests her forehead on her desk. "First, why this program? Why this event? What are we *actually* trying to accomplish... and is a party even the right way to do it?"

She pings the COO.

Lauren: "If the goal is morale and trust, a ballroom won't fix broken habits. Should we confirm the desired outcome before we book a DJ?"

COO: "Fair. What do you propose?"

Lauren: "Define the outcome, then choose the format. If we want to foster true belonging and heartfelt recognition, we need to showcase employee voices and customer proof, not rinky-dink trophies."

Once the lightbulb goes on and they clarify the desired outcome, they quickly align on an in-person event as the right fit: real-time energy for recognition, cross-team connections that build stronger working relationships, and customer shout-outs that land best face-to-face. Plus, they stream highlights for remote teams and package personalized clips for immediate distribution, so nobody is left out.

She hops on three 30-minute huddles with Employee Resource Group (ERG) leaders and a site lead.

Lauren: "What would make people feel seen, not staged or cringey?"

ERG Lead: "Stories. Quick ones.

And shout-outs from customers who felt the impact."

Site Lead: "And please... no mashed potato bar."

Lauren: "Deal. Potatoes retired."

They co-design a night that truly reflects the workforce. Out goes the popularity contest. In comes a peer-to-peer Values in Action showcase, three 90-second employee stories, and two pre-recorded customer shout-outs. Short. Real. Specific.

Before invites go out, Lauren equips people managers with a five-sentence recognition script and launches an always-on kudos channel that rolls into quarterly spot awards.

Manager: "Do I have to make a speech?"

Lauren: "Nope. Read the script. Name the behavior, name the impact, and say thank you. Done."

People feel seen. The room feels honest. And yes, zero branded water bottles end up in the landfill. Big win.

Recognition + Engagement

**"Many times, it's not what you say.
It's what you did.
Your workers want to see
your kind words in action.
That's how you build trust
over time."**

What it is, simplified.

Recognition marks meaningful effort, behaviors, and results. Engagement keeps people connected to the work, the team, and the mission. When done right, both reinforce your company's values, spark that *they noticed me* feeling, making it super clear what good looks like.

Recognize when people live the company's values, mission, and vision. Name it, appreciate it, and celebrate it with their coworkers and customers. Recognition should be specific, timely, and fair. Name the behavior, recognize it close to the moment, and make sure it is reachable across roles and locations. Build a simple cadence: everyday kudos, milestone moments, and impact awards. Tie each one to outcomes customers will recognize and value.

Start with why (use this two-step filter)

Start with why. Name the outcome first, then pick the approach: program, event, or simple team ritual. In this order, you save budget, time, and sanity. Goodbye, "we've always done it this way." When the why is clear, the what and how snap into focus.

Step one: Why this approach?

Decide whether you need a program, an event, or a team ritual.
* **Program** = ongoing behavior change (e.g., peer-to-peer kudos that rolls up quarterly)
* **Event** = one-time spike of energy, celebration, or storytelling (in-person, virtual, or hybrid, such as an annual showcase with customer shout-outs)
* **Team ritual** = fast, local reinforcement (e.g., Friday wins, demo days, stand-up kudos)

Ask:
* What result are we trying to create?
* Can a simple ritual get us there faster and cheaper?
* Will a live, in-person room create connection we can't get on Slack?
* If virtual, how will we drive interaction through polls, live praise, or breakout stories?

Define success in one sentence, then pick the format that delivers it.

Step two: What change do we want to produce?

Name the feeling and the action.
Ask:
* How do we want people to feel during and after this?

Examples:
* seen and proud
* recharged
* connected across sites
* clear on what good looks like

Ask:
* What do we want them to do during or after this?

Examples:
- use the five-sentence recognition script
- nominate a peer
- try one new customer-value behavior
- share a Values in Action story in team huddles

Make it testable: if we surveyed tomorrow, could people tell us what was celebrated, why it mattered, and what they are doing differently?

Design Lens: Julia Rutherford Silvers, CSEP — The 6 A's of Event Design

With gratitude to Julia Rutherford Silvers, who passed on April 27, 2020. We honor her 6 A's framework as a simple way to design an impactful recognition moment, regardless of budget size as a live event, an online event, or as a hybrid function:
- **Anticipation:** What pre-event communication builds excitement and sets clear expectations?
- **Arrival:** How do people feel welcomed in the first few moments, whether on-site or virtual?
- **Atmosphere:** Does the tone, pacing, and production fit your values? Visualize the experience with all five senses.
- **Appetite:** Are food, breaks, and timing inclusive and practical for all shifts and dietary needs?
- **Activities:** Are there short, meaningful moments where employees and customers tell the story? Can you add a spark of fun or collaboration that fits the goal?
- **Amenities:** What small touches show that the organization cares, such as accessibility, translation, childcare notes, opt-in swag, or thoughtful small gifts?

Why it matters now

Shallow perks don't move the needle. Specific, fair, and timely recognition does.

It builds belonging, strengthens trust in managers, and lifts performance because people can see and feel their impact. It also lowers regretted attrition by showing people that their effort matters.

When you anchor recognition to your values and to moments customers truly appreciate, culture compounds in the right direction. When you anchor it to swag or popularity, cynicism compounds just as fast.

Pick receipts over trinkets. Always.

Common mistakes & pitfalls (so you can avoid them)

Mistake

Solution

Mistake	Solution
Popularity contests and "Employee of the Month" awards	Replace them with peer-nominated, values-based recognition tied to observable behaviors and outcomes. Ask: How did they embody our core values in their work?
Vague praise ("Great job!")	Use a specific, behavior-based script that names the action, the impact, and the core value it reflects.
HQ-only programs that ignore frontline, retail, or remote workers	Make it channel-agnostic: in-person and virtual shout-outs, shift-friendly rituals, and translated communications for multi-lingual employees.
Big annual gala, zero day-to-day moments	Layer daily or weekly micro-recognition moments with quarterly showcases and milestone awards. Empower peers to recognize one another through a simple platform or team ritual.
One-size-fits-all rewards	Offer choice: time, growth, money, or visibility. Small budget, big meaning. Make it timely, specific, and employee-chosen, like a one-hour early finish, a $25 course credit, or a public shout-out that actually helps them gain visibility.
Set-it-and-forget-it programs	Run quarterly tune-ups with ERGs and site reps. Review equity and reach, then decide what to refine and what to retire.

One simple tip — #DoTheThing (this week)

Adopt this five-sentence recognition script. Share it with every people manager today.

Five-sentence script:

1. "I saw you [specific action]."
2. "It mattered because [impact on team/customer]."
3. "It reflects our value of [value name]."
4. "Keep doing more of [behavior]."
5. "How can I remove a roadblock so this is easier next time?"

30-day recognition + engagement sprint

Days 1–3: Frame the why

Define the outcome, audience, and constraints. Write success in one sentence.

Days 4–6: Co-design

Run three 30-minute huddles with ERG and site representatives. List 10 ideas. Pick three that fit the goals and budget.

Days 7–10: Build the system

Launch an always-on kudos channel. Publish the five-sentence script. Create a simple peer-nomination form with value, behavior, impact, and a link to proof.

Days 11–15: Pilot recognition moments

Have two team stand-ups use the script. Add one customer-read shout-out per week. Capture short clips.

Days 16–20: Quarterly showcase

Host a 25-minute live or virtual segment: three peer stories, one customer thank-you, and one manager lightning round.

Days 21–24: Reward menu

Offer choice: half-day off, conference credit, mentoring coffee with a VP, spotlight story, or small bonus.

Days 25–27: Equity check

Review participation by location, shift, role, and identity group. Close gaps quickly.

Days 28–30: Close the loop

Publish: what we recognized, why it mattered, and what's next. Retire one low-value ritual.

Momentum moves (how to scale in impactful ways)

Three tiers, clear purpose

Day-to-day kudos for speed, quarterly impact showcases for story and customer voice, and annual milestone awards for service and outsized outcomes.

Peer-to-peer gravity

Use values-based nominations that require evidence. Make them simple to submit from mobile.

Manager enablement

Give managers a 10-minute micro-training and a cheat sheet. Add one weekly calendar nudge to prompt real-time praise.

Customer voice

Invite a customer to read a 60-second thank-you for the team that solved a real problem.

Choice-based rewards

Let winners choose from growth, time, money, or visibility. Publish the menu.

Quarterly tune-up

Review reach and equity with ERGs. Retire one stale element every quarter.

METRICS THAT MATTER

Recognition + Engagement Metrics	What It Tells You
% of employees recognized monthly	Breadth. Aim for steady reach across roles, sites, and at all levels.
Time to recognition (days from act to praise)	Freshness. Faster is better.
"Recognition is specific and fair" (Top-2 box)	Quality signal from the pulse.
Participation by segment	Equity across frontline, remote, HQ, and shifts.
Retention of recognized employees vs. baseline	Whether recognized employees are staying at higher rates than the baseline.
Manager usage of the script	Whether the recognition script is becoming part of regular manager behavior. Spot low-adoption pockets and coach accordingly.
Recognition distribution (HiPo vs. org baseline) *(internal audit)*	Fairness. Compare the share of recognitions going to HiPos against their share of headcount. Investigate if it over-indexes by more than 1.5× for two or more months.
Coverage parity by segment vs. baseline *(internal audit)*	Reach equity. Are underrepresented groups, frontline workers, and new hires with fewer than 180 days receiving recognition at similar rates?
Manager concentration index *(internal audit)*	Attention spread. Are roughly 10% of people getting about 50% of kudos? Rebalance if yes.
Outcome-alignment check *(internal audit)*	Integrity. Sample quarterly. Does each recognition cite a value and a specific impact? Track the yes/no rate.

Tip: *Publish the first six metrics. Keep the four internal-audit metrics for coaching and fairness checks.*

Using AI to simplify (Recognition + Engagement)

Use Case	Good Prompt	Even Better Prompt
Draft values-based kudos	"Write praise for great teamwork."	"You are a People Ops partner with 10+ years of experience. Draft a five-sentence kudos message using our script for an employee who coordinated a cross-team handoff that saved a customer renewal. Value: 'Own the outcome.' Keep it specific and human."
Create a peer-nomination form	"Make a nomination form."	"Create a one-page peer-nomination form for 'Values in Action.' Include these fields: nominee, value, behavior, impact on customer/team, and link to proof. Add a plain-English privacy note and examples."
Quarterly showcase agenda	"Plan a recognition event."	"Draft a 25-minute recognition showcase agenda with three peer stories (90 seconds each), one customer thank-you (60 seconds), and one manager lightning panel (three questions). Include a host script and transitions."
Equity review snapshot	"Analyze who got awards."	"Given this CSV of recognitions by site, role, shift, and ERG, flag under-reached groups and suggest three targeted interventions. Return a short brief."
Bias and privacy check	"Check this for issues."	"Act as a bias and privacy checker. Highlight any identifying medical information, protected traits, or loaded language in these nominations. Propose neutral rewrites."

Quick AI guardrails reminder:

- Strip names and any personally identifiable information (PII) before pasting content into AI. This includes anything confidential, sensitive, or internal-only.
- Treat outputs as "dirty first drafts." A human should always review, proofread, and own the final wording and decisions.
- Use AI to speed up the writing, not to replace judgment. Check every output for bias, hallucinations, tone issues, and factual errors.
- Keep recognition specific, fair, and grounded in real behavior and impact. If AI adds exaggeration or any sort of generic praise, rewrite it.
- Log what AI touched for transparency.

REAL-WORLD CASE STUDY

Making Appreciation Meaningful at Work

Recognition programs often fail for a simple reason. They are designed around what leaders like to give, not how employees actually feel valued.

Dr. Paul White, psychologist and co-author of *The 5 Languages of Appreciation in the Workplace: Empowering Organizations by Encouraging People*, has spent decades studying why recognition efforts miss the mark. His research revealed a clear disconnect. Many organizations invest in formal recognition programs, yet employee engagement and morale often remain flat. The issue is not effort. It is misalignment.

The Challenge: Generic Recognition Feels Invisible

Dr. White found that many employees go a full year without receiving any meaningful appreciation. Not because leaders do not care, but because appreciation is delivered in ways that do not resonate. A public award, a generic "good job," or a company-branded gift can feel hollow if it is not aligned with what the individual actually values.

Leaders often assume recognition is universally motivating. In reality, people experience appreciation differently. When recognition misses its target, it does not feel neutral. It feels non-existent.

The Strategy: Personalize Appreciation Without Making It Overly Complicated

Dr. White and his colleague Dr. Gary Chapman adapted the well-known '5 Love Languages' framework for the workplace, identifying five distinct ways people *prefer* to receive appreciation at work. The key insight is simple. Not everyone feels valued in the same way. Most people have one or two languages that matter most.

The 5 Languages of Appreciation at Work include:

- **Words of affirmation**: Specific, sincere verbal or written praise that highlights what someone did well and why it mattered. Tip: Ask whether they prefer this privately or publicly.
- **Quality time**: Feeling valued through focused time together, whether one-on-one conversations, lunch together, or meaningful connection with colleagues.
- **Acts of service**: Appreciation shown by helping lighten someone's workload or stepping in to support them.
- **Gifts**: Thoughtful, personal items that show you've paid attention to their personal preferences versus giving generic swag.
- **Touch**: Appropriate gestures like a high five, fist bump, handshake, or a pat on the back in moments of shared success.

The power of this framework is not perfection, it's intention. Leaders do not need to do everything for everyone. They just need to do the right thing for each person.

The Outcome: Stronger Engagement Through Being Seen

When appreciation is personalized, employees feel seen rather than managed. That is where trust grows. Dr. White's research shows that feeling valued directly impacts retention, morale, productivity, and profitability. Recognition shifts from performative to personal.

The lesson is clear. Appreciation is not about grand gestures or expensive programs. It is about understanding people, appreciating their efforts along the way, and responding accordingly.

Practical Lessons for HR and People Leaders

- Generic recognition often misses the mark. Personalization matters.
- Ask how people prefer to be appreciated instead of assuming.
- Small, specific actions can have an incredible, positive impact.

Remember, appreciation works when it reflects how people actually feel valued, not how leaders think it should look.

The 7-minute reality check
(Recognition + Engagement)

Set a timer for seven minutes. Be blunt. Be concrete.

1. **Where are we praising loudly but vaguely?** Write three real examples and rewrite one using the script.

2. **Who gets missed?** Name one location, shift, or role that rarely shows up in recognition. Plan one fix and be specific.

3. **Which ritual should we retire this quarter?** Name it and explain why.

4. **What would a customer thank us for this month?** How do we bring that voice in?

5. **If we had no budget, how would we still make people feel seen next week?**

JOT DOWN
YOUR IDEAS
HERE

FIND
BONUS
RESOURCES
HERE

Choose-your-own-adventure

- Need a quick breathing exercise to find your calm? Head to page 289.
- Need a spark of creativity to get your brain going? Head to page 290.
- Need a refresh on employee listening? Head to page 19.
- Want to take action on your new hire onboarding process?
  Head to the next chapter.

You just rebuilt recognition from performative to powerful: clear purpose, honest stories, daily habits, and proof that people matter. Well done, you.

Next, let's make sure your new hires feel this from day one, and do not regret accepting that job offer.

Are you ready?

Let's dive in.

It's time to simplify: **New Hire Onboarding That Feels Like Belonging.**

The Simplifiers Employee Experience Flywheel™

NEW HIRE
ONBOARDING

7

New Hire Onboarding That Feels Like Belonging

*"A paycheck may bring people in the door.
Trust is what helps them stay."*

—Mary

Never again to the sad desk lunch

On her first day many years ago, Lauren didn't know where to park, what to wear, or where to sit. The desk had someone else's nameplate. She ate a sad bologna sandwich all by herself and questioned her life choices.

"Is this... the break room or a supply closet?" she whispered to no one.

Flash forward to today. Now she owns onboarding.

She fixes the mess with a simple vow: never again.

In her first attempt, she overcorrects and blasts a 40-page PDF before Day 1. New hires reply, "Yikes. I wasn't expecting a pop quiz." Oof.

She catches it, opens this playbook, and simplifies: a five-minute welcome video, a mobile-friendly parking map, tips on what to wear, and a simple checklist.

From there, she launches a cross-functional welcome cohort. She trains new hire buddies to send a 60-second intro video. She sets a standing "no one lunches alone" table at every site. IT ships gear early and includes a sticky note with the Wi-Fi and first login.

"You're not allowed to hunt for passwords," she jokes.

Managers get a clean 30/60/90-day onboarding plan and a one-page check-in agenda.

The result? Day 1 feels human. Week 1 builds clarity. By Week 4, every new hire ships a small win they can feel proud of.

Time to productivity improves. New-hire regret drops on the pulse. And the sad desk lunch? Retired.

New Hire Onboarding

"You don't get a second chance to make an excellent first impression. Why spend so much time, money, effort and resources attracting the very best talent to stumble on day one?"

What it is, simplified.

Onboarding turns a new person into a confident teammate.

It delivers three signals early and often:

- **Confidence** — *I can do this.*
- **Clarity** — *I know what good looks like.*
- **Connection** — *These are my people.*

It aligns the manager, the new hire buddy, and the new hire around the same outcomes, so every touchpoint moves in the same direction.

It also removes friction fast: logins work, tools are ready, and the first win is small, visible, and tied to real customer value.

But here's the thing: it starts before day one, in the pre-boarding phase.

That's the time between accepting the offer and stepping into the role. This critical window sets many signals in motion and helps new hires feel like they made the right decision. Get this phase right if you want to retain top talent, nurture performance, and build belonging.

The arc from pre-boarding to Day 90 looks like this:

Prepare →
Welcome →
Learn →
Ship →
Grow.

Why it matters now

Miss this window and you pay later in churn, rework, and disengagement. Done well, onboarding cuts time to effectiveness, builds trust in managers, and lowers early attrition.

It also reframes the job in the new hire's mind.

For high-volume roles that can feel like just a paycheck, show how the work will positively impact real customer outcomes and offer clear steps to advance within the organization. Show people the leadership development path they can own.

For dream jobs, make the runway concrete with a first win, a dedicated new hire buddy to show them the ropes, and a thoughtful 30/60/90-day action plan that genuinely excites them. This is how you turn empty promises into real progress.

Your goal is to help every new hire see this role as a smart next step in their career. Here, they are valuable, goals are achievable, and the work is worth their best effort.

Common mistakes & pitfalls (so you can avoid them)

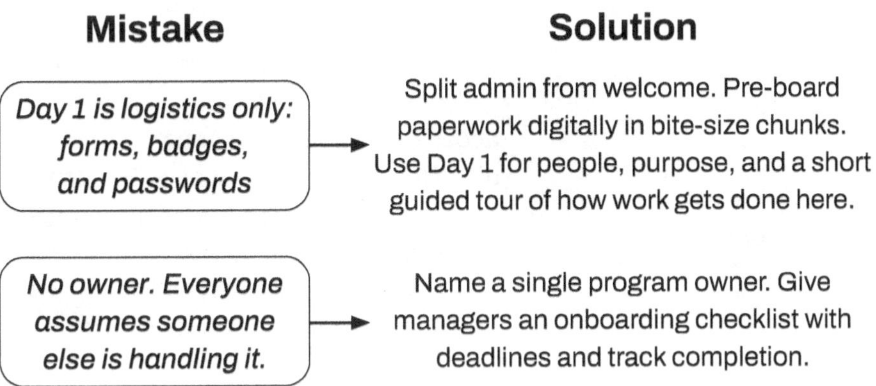

(continued)

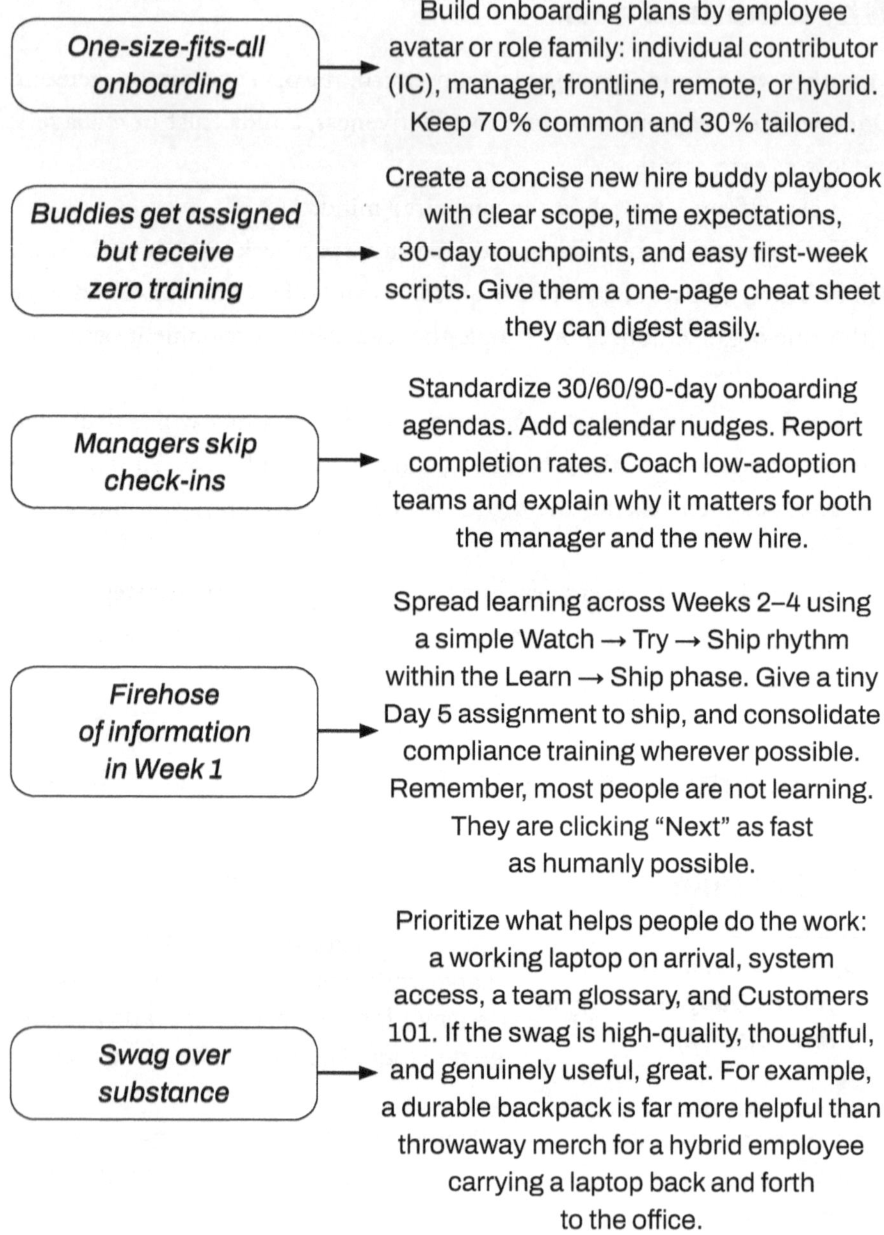
One-size-fits-all onboarding
Build onboarding plans by employee avatar or role family: individual contributor (IC), manager, frontline, remote, or hybrid. Keep 70% common and 30% tailored.
Buddies get assigned but receive zero training
Create a concise new hire buddy playbook with clear scope, time expectations, 30-day touchpoints, and easy first-week scripts. Give them a one-page cheat sheet they can digest easily.
Managers skip check-ins
Standardize 30/60/90-day onboarding agendas. Add calendar nudges. Report completion rates. Coach low-adoption teams and explain why it matters for both the manager and the new hire.
Firehose of information in Week 1
Spread learning across Weeks 2–4 using a simple Watch → Try → Ship rhythm within the Learn → Ship phase. Give a tiny Day 5 assignment to ship, and consolidate compliance training wherever possible. Remember, most people are not learning. They are clicking "Next" as fast as humanly possible.
Swag over substance
Prioritize what helps people do the work: a working laptop on arrival, system access, a team glossary, and Customers 101. If the swag is high-quality, thoughtful, and genuinely useful, great. For example, a durable backpack is far more helpful than throwaway merch for a hybrid employee carrying a laptop back and forth to the office.

Remember, there are four questions every new hire wants answered before day one:

In-person or Hybrid Employee	Remote Employee
Where do I park and enter?	When do I log on, and how do I access tools like VPN, email, chat, and calendar?
What do I wear?	What do I wear?
Who am I meeting upon arrival, and where?	Who am I meeting first, and how? Include the link.
Who am I having lunch with, and where?	When should I break for lunch?

Once the background check clears, send a Day 1 Snapshot email three business days before they start. Keep it simple, clear, and thoughtful. Include:

- answers to the four questions
- the first-day agenda
- names and photos of key people
- any setup steps

Get this right and your day five pulse will likely skew positive. Surprises sink confidence. Clarity builds it.

Let's make a great first impression.

One simple tip — #DoTheThing (this week)

Pick one open role, or req. Draft a 30-day onboarding plan for that role, including:

- five people to meet
- three systems to access
- one tiny assignment to ship by Day 10
- one 30-minute buddy touchpoint scheduled each week

Put it on the calendar before they start.

Remember, you can upload the job description into AI and have it help you build the first draft of the onboarding plan. No need to start from scratch.

30-day new hire onboarding sprint

Days 1–3: Frame and assign

Name an onboarding owner. Pick the first two employee avatars to pilot, such as SDR and Software Engineer. Draft a 90-day arc for each avatar: pre-board, Day 1, Week 1, Weeks 2–4, and Weeks 5–12. Select and train 10–15 buddies across sites or office locations, with clear expectations, time commitments, and scripts.

Days 4–6: Pre-boarding

Send the welcome pack: parking, dress norms, Day-1 agenda, team map, first-week goals, laptop delivery or pickup, manager welcome note, and buddy intro. Confirm system access for Day 1.

Days 7–9: Day-1 experience

Run a 60–90-minute welcome covering purpose, values in action, and customers in plain English. Give a tour of the office or virtual environment and introduce key people. Host a team lunch or virtual coffee. Set the tiny ship, a small real task due by Day 10. Spread out compliance training so it is not overwhelming. End the day with a manager check-in: "What's unclear? What questions do you have?"

Days 10–14: Week-1 rhythm

Run daily 15-minute stand-ups with the manager or buddy: "What is your focus today? What questions do you have? What roadblocks can I help remove?" Cover the basics of how work gets done here: tools, rituals, decision rights, and the glossary of acronyms. Finish the tiny ship and share it at the Friday huddle.

Days 15–20: Weeks 2–3

Move into Watch → Try → Ship blocks tied to role outcomes. Add a Customers 101 experience: shadow a call, ticket, or demo. Hold a 30-minute manager check-in on wins, questions, and the next two ships. Ask: "What do you need more of, or less of, from me?"

Days 21–30: Week 4 and beyond

Assign a second ship with a little more scope. Run a mini peer-feedback loop on what helped and what remains unclear. Publish the 30/60/90-day action plan and schedule the coaching touchpoints.

Momentum moves
(how to scale this across your org)

Welcome cohorts: Monthly groups across functions to build peer connections. Add a 60-day reunion to share first wins and one interesting thing learned about the organization.

Buddy network: Match by employee avatar and site location. Rotate quarterly. Recognize effective buddies and have them mentor new buddies.

Role maps: Create one-page guides showing what good looks like, key tool links, and common pitfalls by role family.

Customer roadshow: Build short evergreen videos from Sales, Support, and Operations. Help new hires understand how value is created before they are asked to innovate it.

Manager enablement: Give managers a 10-minute prep kit for each new hire: scripts, timelines, and the 30/60/90-day onboarding checklist. Make it super simple for them to use these tools.

Career site update: Show your onboarding arc publicly to prospective talent. Set honest expectations and attract better-fit candidates over time.

METRICS THAT MATTER

New Hire Onboarding Metrics	What It Tells You
Time to first ship (in days)	How fast a new hire delivers a first visible win.
Time to effectiveness (days to baseline outcomes)	When they consistently hit the agreed outcomes for the role.
New-hire Net Promoter Score (NPS) at Day 30 and Day 90	Confidence and satisfaction early on. Did reality match the promise?
30/60/90 completion rate (manager & new hire)	Whether structured check-ins are actually happening.
Buddy touchpoint completion (weekly in first month)	Whether the support system is working when it matters most.
6-month and 12-month regretted attrition	Whether you are losing people you wanted to keep.
Access on Day 1 (all systems ready)	Basic friction: did tools and logins work from the start?

Pick three to four to publish each month. Keep the set stable so you can see the trend lines.

Using AI to simplify (New Hire Onboarding)

Use Case	Good Prompt	Even Better Prompt
Draft a 90-day onboarding arc	"Create a 90-day onboarding plan for a Customer Success Manager."	"You are an expert onboarding designer. Create a 90-day plan for a Customer Success Manager in B2B SaaS using this framework: Prepare → Welcome → Learn → Ship → Grow. Include a pre-boarding checklist, Day-1 agenda, Week-1 goals across people, product, and process, Watch → Try → Ship blocks for Weeks 2–4, and Weeks 5–12 milestones with two small ships. Keep it in plain English. Return it as a one-page checklist."
Buddy playbook	"Write a buddy guide."	"Write a one-page buddy playbook for a remote Software Engineer. This person will act as an approachable ambassador for the new hire, someone they can ask 'dumb questions' and learn the unwritten rules from. Include purpose, time expectations (30 minutes per week for four weeks), a first-week script, what to escalate, and a quick debrief form. Keep it friendly and specific."
Manager 30/60/90	"Make a 30/60/90 template."	"Create a 30/60/90-day action plan template for a Sales Development Rep. Include three outcomes per phase, sample ships, meeting cadence, and a 20-minute check-in agenda. Add a field for risks and roadblocks."
Role glossary	"Write a team glossary."	"Draft a team glossary for Product Marketing with no more than 25 terms or acronyms. For each one, include a one-sentence definition and a link placeholder. Keep the tone clear and non-jargony. If the information is not yet known, create a short interview script that will help pull it from a stakeholder."

Welcome note	"Write a welcome email."	"Write a warm 150-word manager welcome note for a new Data Analyst. Mention the buddy intro, first-day agenda, answers to the four key questions, and the Day-10 tiny ship. Keep the tone human, specific, and free of filler."

Quick AI guardrails reminder:

- Strip names and any personally identifiable information (PII) before pasting content into AI. This includes anything confidential, internal-only, or not meant to be shared outside your organization.
- Treat outputs as "dirty first drafts." A human should always review, proofread, and own the final wording, decisions, and promises.
- Use AI to speed up drafts, checklists, and structure, not to invent onboarding details your team cannot actually deliver.
- Review every output for bias, inaccessible language, hallucinations, and operational errors before anything goes live.
- Log what AI touched for transparency.

REAL-WORLD CASE STUDY

Bringing Connection Back Into Onboarding

While serving as a **Leadership & Employee Development Consultant at Southwest Airlines, Spencer Gentry** saw firsthand how culture can feel different when onboarding goes fully remote. He understood that those earliest moments in an employee's journey matter more than most organizations realize and are willing to invest in. They set the stage and chart the course for everything that follows in the employee's career.

The Challenge: When Onboarding Loses the Human Touch

Like many organizations, when Southwest shifted onboarding online during the pandemic, new hires got the essentials, but not the connection. Spencer described it as "a couple hours online," focused mostly on need-to-knows like technical basics and benefits, with only "a little piece of culture and history." He said it felt more like "an onboarding class" instead of a full orientation experience. Facilitators were strong, but the format felt rushed, cameras were often off, and people were not able to connect with other new hires.

Many employees hired during that period also missed key experiences that had long been part of Southwest's culture, including meeting people from other departments, seeing headquarters, and receiving the signature Red Carpet Welcome, where employees are enthusiastically cheered on by their new Cohearts* (*that's what they call their colleagues) as they walk down a long red carpet. These iconic moments that created immediate belonging were gone.

Over time, feedback made it clear that many employees felt they had missed out on something meaningful.

The Strategy: Reconnect People to Culture on Purpose

To close that gap, Southwest created the Southwest Airlines Campus Experience for employees who had been hired during that period and never got that in-person introduction to the culture. Spencer, who owned the Now Onboarding program, described his role as the "spider in a web," making sure all the pieces came together across key stakeholders and vendors.

The team built a half-day experience and flew participants to its Dallas headquarters, a pretty great perk of being an airline. They focused on what employees had missed most: the Red Carpet Welcome, time with a senior leader, opportunities to connect with Cohearts from other departments and locations, and a campus tour. The goal was not to repeat information people already had. It was to help them reconnect with the organization in "a more intentional and meaningful way."

Spencer said the Campus Experience reinforced a simple message for employees who had been hired remotely: Southwest didn't just value them on day one, they valued them years into their journey.

The Outcome: High Demand and Stronger Connection

The response was immediate and enthusiastic. Southwest initially scheduled three or four Campus Experiences during the summer. However, demand was so high with long waitlists, they nearly doubled the session offerings to accommodate all who wanted to participate. The broader in-person Now Onboarding experience also showed strong results, with satisfaction increasing about 15 percentage points to more than 90%.

For Spencer, though, the biggest measure of success was emotional:

"They will forever remember how they felt on their first day."

That became his filter for every improvement to the onboarding program. If the experience helped people feel connected to the organization, the people, and the culture, then it was worth doing.

Practical Lessons for HR & People Leaders

- Onboarding should create connection, not just transfer information. It should help people feel seen and welcomed, not just informed.
- Visible culture moments matter. Experiences like Southwest's Red Carpet Welcome make appreciation feel real.
- Listen fast and refine faster. The strongest onboarding programs evolve continuously based on employee feedback.

The bigger lesson is simple: when people feel welcomed, cared for, and appreciated from the start, they carry that feeling into the work that follows.

The 7-minute reality check
(New Hire Onboarding)

Set a timer for seven minutes and jot down quick answers. This will help spark ideas about what to tackle first.

1. **What confused you on your last Day 1 that you can remove for the next hire?**

2. **Do new hires ship anything in the first 10 business days?** If not, what is the smallest real task you can assign?

3. **Are manager check-ins on the calendar now?** Are 30/60/90-day check-ins scheduled, complete with agendas?

4. **Do the assigned buddies know what's expected of them?** Write the first-week talking points.

5. **Is system access ready on arrival?** List the blockers and owners.

JOT DOWN YOUR IDEAS HERE

FIND BONUS RESOURCES HERE

Choose-your-own-adventure

- Need a pep talk from Mary? Head to page 291.
- Need a quick laugh before you lose your ish? Head to page 292.
- Need a refresh on employee listening? Head to page 19.
- Want to take action on your organization's digital employee experience? Head to the next chapter.

You've rebuilt Day 1 through Day 90 so new hires feel confident, clear, and connected. Now ask yourself: what would make you feel truly welcomed and like you belong here?

What small signals would quiet that fear, *Did I pick the wrong job?*, before it takes root?

Now comes the quiet multiplier: the digital stuff people touch every hour. If logins fail, search returns junk, or "How do I...?" turns into a time-wasting scavenger hunt, even the best onboarding starts to leak trust.

Next up, we clean the pipes.

We'll audit the tech stack for friction and findability, set simple content rules so the intranet stays fresh, and design help paths that get people unstuck fast. Not very techy? No sweat. We'll also turn generative AI into a safe desk mate for FAQs, drafts, and guided navigation, with privacy and bias checks built in.

Are you ready?

Let's dive in.

It's time to simplify: **The Digital Employee Experience (That Isn't From 1986).**

The Simplifiers Employee Experience Flywheel™

DIGITAL
EMPLOYEE
EXPERIENCE

8

The Digital Employee Experience (That Isn't From 1986)

"When people cannot find what they need, do what they need, or trust the tools they use, performance suffers. "

—Mary

LEARN FROM LAUREN

Two hamsters, one intranet (and a truce)

"Where's the vacation policy?" Lauren searches.

Result: a 2019 PDF and a 404 error. Great.

She meets with IT.

IT lead: "The intranet works. People just don't use it right." Engineer: "Nav's from 2018. Classic."

Lauren slows it down.

Lauren: "You built for security and compliance. Makes sense. Can we watch how it lands today?"

She plays three 60-second clips of employees hunting for time-off, leave, and expense answers. Click... stall... quit.

Engineer: "Oof."

Lauren: "How about this? No need to rebuild a brand-new platform. Let's make one front door and ten great pages."

IT lead: "Then we'll drown in content requests."

Lauren: "You keep the platform. We'll train the page owners, and I'll create the templates and track the quarterly review dates so nothing turns into zombie content."

She slides across a one-pager:

- **Front door:** five top tasks
- **Templates:** task guide, policy in plain English, FAQ
- **Governance:** owner + review date, or auto-archive
- **Search:** pin correct answers; add synonyms
- **AI concierge (pilot):** approved sources + citations
- **Goal:** 40% faster answers for the top 10 tasks in 30 business days

Engineer: "I can pin results by Friday."

IT lead: "Loop Legal in on 'plain English.'"

Lauren: "Who's in the sprint so this is yours too?"

IT lead: "Me, Priya from Security, and Sam from Search. You bring HR and Support stewards. And snacks."

They form the DEX Squad, short for Digital Employee Experience.

Week 1: archive 600 stale pages, pin answers, and launch the "How do I...?" home page.

Week 2: add citations and set review dates.

IT lead: "Okay, but this was our idea."

Lauren: "Exactly."

Tickets drop. Customer Satisfaction Score (CSAT) climbs. Hamsters retired.

Lauren has now mastered the art of speaking geek and letting them believe it was their idea all along.

The Digital Employee Experience (DEX)

"If your tools make people want to poke their eyes out just to find a simple answer, you've got a problem."

What it is, simplified.

DEX is how work moves through your systems: Find → Do → Move On.

Good DEX makes answers obvious, tasks fast, and errors rare. Ownership is shared:

- **IT or HR IT:** owns the platforms
- **HR / People Ops:** owns policies and tasks
- **Internal Communications**: owns language and findability
- **Page owners:** own the content

In smaller organizations, that may be one person wearing multiple hats, and that's okay. You are still in a pivotal position to humanize the tools and improve the online employee experience in real, visible ways.

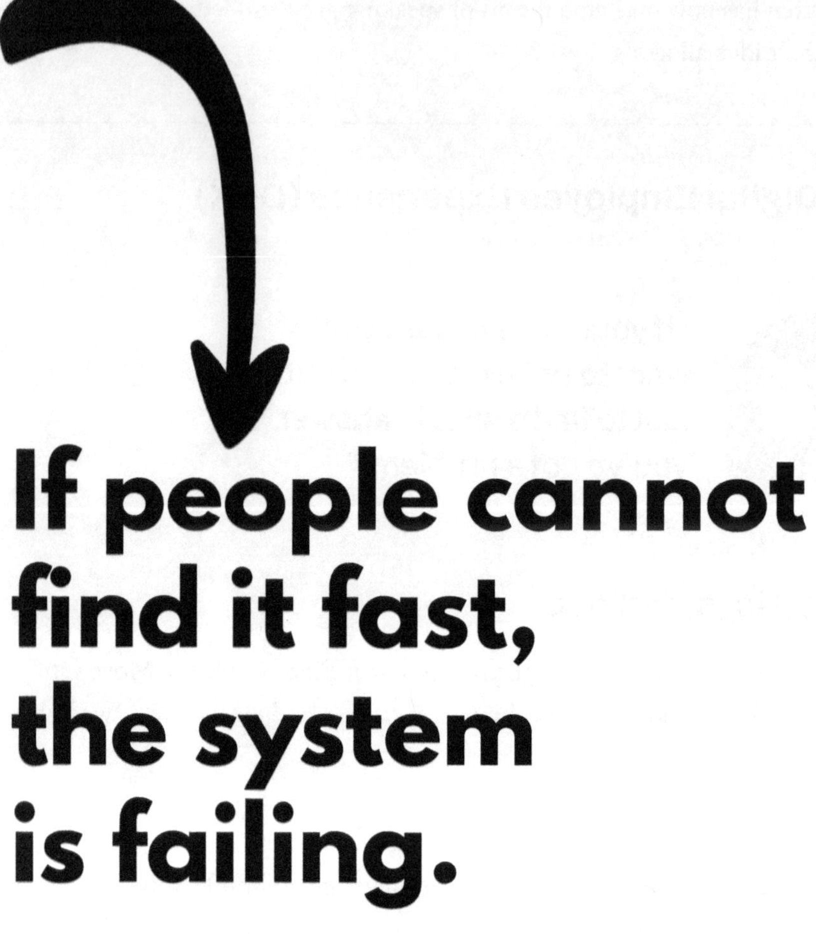
If people cannot find it fast, the system is failing.

How to influence it: show the pain with data, such as task time, clicks to answer, and employee satisfaction ratings. Replay short usability clips and run a 30-day pilot on the top 10 tasks. Pin the right answers. Use plain-English pages. Set review dates. Track whether time to answer drops.

You do not need more tools. You need clearer paths, fresher content, and simple governance.

Why it matters now

Every minute spent hunting for "How do I...?" is a minute not spent serving our customers.

Bad DEX creates shadow channels, duplicate work, burnout, and avoidable tickets. Put simply, it wastes everyone's time.

Fixing DEX lifts productivity, builds trust, and increases adoption of the systems you already pay for.

The pattern is simple: make the front door obvious, keep the content true, and measure task time, not clicks.

Common mistakes & pitfalls (so you can avoid them)

Mistake	Solution
"This new tool will save us."	Start with an audit. What is the current tech stack workflow? Remove duplicative tools. Improve information architecture and search before adding software.
No single entry point	Create one visible "How do I...?" front door. Route people to tasks, not pages. Reduce the number of clicks it takes to get to the right answer.
Search returns junk	Add synonyms, pin top results, and de-index stale pages. Review top queries monthly.
Zombie content (stale or conflicting)	Set page owners, review dates, and an archive policy. Pages with no owner get archived.
Policy language is legalese	Publish a plain-language version with a short FAQ. Link the legal PDF for reference.
DIY sprawl, where anyone can publish	Require owners, templates, and approvals for key spaces. Train 10% of the organization as content stewards.
Help paths stall	Offer three paths: self-serve guide, step-by-step task, or "talk to a human," with clear response-time expectations.
No metrics	Track task time, errors, and satisfaction. Use the data to choose the next fixes.

One simple tip — #DoTheThing (this week)

Pick the top 10 "How do I...?" questions from tickets or chat.

Write 10 one-page answers in plain language, each with a short step list, screenshots, and a "Need help?" section at the end.

Then pin them to the front door of your site and track whether support tickets start to drop over the next 14 days.

30-day digital employee experience sprint

Days 1–3: Frame

Name a DEX owner and a five-person squad: HRIS, IT, Support, one manager, and one individual contributor. Define success in one sentence: "Reduce time to answer for the top 10 tasks by 40%."

Days 4–7: Audit

Inventory your systems: HRIS, LMS, intranet, collaboration tools, ticketing, and messaging. Pull the top search queries and the top ticket types. Note duplicates and dead links.

Days 8–11: Design

Map a new front door with five to seven big buttons: Pay / Time, Time Off, Benefits, Careers, Policies, IT Help. Draft templates for:

- Task
- Policy in plain English
- FAQ
- Decision memo

Days 12–16: Build

Launch the front door. Create or fix the top 10 pages. Add "last reviewed" and page owner labels. Configure search pins and synonyms. De-index stale content.

Days 17–19: AI concierge (pilot)

Add a governed chatbot for policy lookups. Scope it to approved sources only. Turn on guardrails: source citations, privacy filter, and feedback button.

Days 20–22: Help paths

Add a "Need a person?" button with Service Level Agreements (SLAs) and queue ownership. Publish a simple "when to escalate" guide.

Days 23–26: Train

Run a 30-minute steward training on templates, tone, and review cycles. Hold a 15-minute manager huddle to show the front door and ask people to bookmark it.

Days 27–30: Measure and iterate

Capture time to answer for the top 10 tasks. Note drops, errors, and feedback. Publish a one-page "You Said / We Shipped" update. Name the next five fixes.

Momentum moves
(scale it across your enterprise, simply)

Front door everywhere: Pin "How do I...?" in the app launcher, Slack or Teams, and email footers.

Steward network: Train 10% of the organization as content stewards. Hold a monthly 30-minute review to reinforce training.

Sunset calendar: Auto-remind owners at 90 days. No owner? Archive it.

Task over page: Design for the job to be done, request, change, enroll, not the department.

Quarterly time-to-answer review: Pick the next five tasks based on time saved and ticket volume.

METRICS THAT MATTER

DEX Metrics	What It Tells You
Task time (minutes) for top 10 tasks	Speed. Are common tasks getting faster?
First-result success rate (%)	Findability. Did search deliver the right answer?
Ticket deflection (%) on top 10 tasks	Self-serve effectiveness.
CSAT for help interactions	Quality of help when self-serve fails.
Content freshness (% of pages in SLA)	Governance health.
AI answer accuracy (with sources)	Trustworthiness of the concierge.

Pick three to four to publish monthly. Keep the set stable so you can see trend lines over time.

Using AI to simplify (The Digital Employee Experience)

Use Case	Good Prompt	Even Better Prompt
Draft a task guide	"Write how to request PTO."	"You are a Digital Employee Experience writer. Create a one-page 'Request PTO' guide for hourly and salaried employees. Include who is eligible, step-by-step instructions in HRIS, the approval timeline, and a link placeholder. Use plain English. Add a mini-FAQ with three common edge cases."
Plain-language policy	"Summarize our leave policy."	"Rewrite this parental leave policy in plain English for employees. Keep the legal terms intact in a linked section. Include eligibility, how to apply, timelines, pay, and who to contact. Add a six-step checklist."
Search synonyms	"Give search terms for benefits."	"List 25 common synonyms and misspellings employees use for 'benefits' and 'health insurance' for search tuning. Return the result as a CSV file with term and canonical tag."
FAQ from tickets	"Make an FAQ."	"From these 100 ticket subjects, cluster the top 10 questions. Write one clear answer per cluster with three-step guidance and a 'talk to a human' link. Flag any policy gaps."
Screenshot walkthrough	"Write steps."	"Create a step-by-step guide for 'change tax withholding' with numbered steps and screenshot captions. Add a warning for common errors and a success check at the end."

Quick AI guardrails reminder:

- Strip names and any personally identifiable information (PII) before pasting content into AI. This includes anything confidential, internal-only, or not meant to be shared outside your organization.
- Treat outputs as "dirty first drafts." A human should always review, proofread, and own the final wording, decisions, and recommendations.
- Use AI to speed up task guides, FAQs, and draft content, not to invent answers your systems, policies, or support teams cannot actually deliver.
- Review every output for bias, hallucinations, broken steps, outdated guidance, and inaccessible language before anything goes live.
- Log what AI touched for transparency.

REAL·WORLD CASE STUDY

Digital Tools That Work for People, Not Against Them

Digital employee experience often fails quietly. Not with a system outage or a headline incident, but through daily friction that slowly erodes trust and productivity.

John Bernatovicz, HR and payroll advocate, entrepreneur, author of *HR Like a Boss and Payroll Like a Boss*, and president of Willory, has seen this pattern repeatedly in his work with organizations navigating technology change. His message is direct: If employees cannot easily use the tools they rely on every day, the problem is not adoption. It is design.

The Challenge: Broken Basics Undermine Trust

John notes that organizations often chase new platforms while overlooking the systems employees touch most. Payroll, time and attendance, and basic

HR transactions are not optional moments. They are trust moments.

When these systems are confusing, unreliable, or slow, employees do not think, *"Gosh, IT is struggling."* They think, *"This company really doesn't care about my time or my pay."* That erosion compounds quickly.

Too often, leaders tolerate poor usability because the system technically works. But "technically working" is different from supporting people in doing their jobs or building their careers.

The Strategy: Fix What Hurts Before Adding What Shines

John emphasizes starting with the highest stakes digital experiences. Payroll must be accurate and easy. Requests like time off, benefits changes, and policy lookups should not require advanced detective work.

He also stresses the importance of understanding the business context. Digital improvements should align with how the company makes money and where employee time matters most. Not every tool deserves equal attention.

Rather than defaulting to buying new software, John advocates improving clarity, workflows, adoption, and ownership inside existing systems first. Small changes in findability, instructions, and accountability can dramatically reduce friction.

The Outcome: Confidence, Efficiency, and Momentum

When digital tools support people instead of slowing them down, employees regain confidence in the organization. Support tickets drop. Frustration eases. The focus returns to real work.

Most importantly, employees feel respected. Their effort is not wasted navigating systems that should be helping them.

Digital employee experience gets better through steady, practical enhancements to the essentials, not flashy tech rollouts. Keep removing friction and confusion, and your workforce will be grateful it did not take twenty-eight clicks to find one simple answer.

Practical Lessons for HR and People Leaders

- If a core system is confusing or unreliable, it is not an IT problem. It is an employee experience problem.
- Start with payroll and other high-stakes moments. Fix the basics before investing in new tools.
- Make decisions with business context. Understand how the company makes money so you can prioritize the right digital fixes.

In the end, great digital employee experience is simple. Make it easy for people to get paid, get answers, and get on with their work.

The 7-minute reality check
(The Digital Employee Experience)

Set a timer for seven minutes. Jot quick answers.

1. **What are the top 10 "How do I...?" questions that employees are asking this quarter? (Ex: How do I submit a vacation request?) Where do they live now?**

2. **How many clicks does it take to request time off, change benefits, or find the holiday calendar?**

3. **Which pages have no clear owner or review date? List three to archive or assign.**

4. **Where does search fail? Type three common queries and note the first result.**

5. **If you had to save 10,000 minutes next month, which three DEX tasks would you fix first?**

**JOT DOWN
YOUR IDEAS
HERE**

**FIND
BONUS
RESOURCES
HERE**

Choose-your-own-adventure

- Need to close a few tabs in your brain and get some headspace?
  Head to page 293.
- Need a pause and want to listen to a guided visualization?
  Head to page 294.
- Need a refresh on employee listening? Head to page 19.
- Want to take action on your organization's workplace experience?
  Head to the next chapter.

Well done. You've cleaned up the clicks. Answers are now easier to find, tasks are faster, and help is one tap away.

Now let's make sure the bricks match the clicks. Yes, I'm talking about your physical office space, what I call workplace experience.

If the office fights the work with bad Wi-Fi, no meeting rooms, and noisy floors, then trust leaks and momentum stalls. Next up, we'll tune the physical space so teams choose the office for what it does best: real collaboration, faster decisions, and energy you can feel.

Are you ready?

Let's dive in.

It's time to simplify: **Workplace Experience — Rethinking the Office for Modern Hybrid Success.**

The Simplifiers Employee Experience Flywheel™

WORKPLACE
EXPERIENCE

9

Workplace Experience: Rethinking the Office Space for Modern Hybrid Success

*"The real question is not where people work.
It is whether the experience helps them work well."*

—Mary

Fix the experience before you mandate the commute

"Okay, the draft return-to-office memo is ready to send," the Chief of Staff to the COO says. "Everyone back in the office, five days a week, starting in two weeks."

Lauren blinks. "Quick question: if 500 people show up on Monday, would our Wi-Fi sputter or just explode?"

IT winces.

Facilities shrugs.

The CHRO whispers, "Hmm, good point. We might also need more meeting rooms."

First things first, Lauren decides to walk the floor with a notebook, and what she sees is wild.

"This sea of desks without privacy walls means everyone, yes, everyone, hears your Zoom calls all the time," she says. "And if we're all wearing headphones blasting lo-fi beats to drown out Karen's legendary cackle, that's not collaboration. That's survival. We can do better. Guys, we've got to do better."

She points at the floor plan. "How are there only six small meeting rooms for an entire building?" she wonders. "Where do squads huddle? Where does a parent take a sensitive call? Where does a designer get two quiet hours to focus in the office?"

Silence.

After a brainstorm with her cross-functional partners and a quick sprint focus group with employees, she identifies the most pressing workspace issues and prioritizes what to improve first.

In the exec room, she lays it out. "If we mandate first and fix later, all we'll gain are disgruntled employees, missed deadlines, and negative Glassdoor reviews from people who bail. If we make these quick fixes first, we'll save ourselves a lot of grief later."

She proposes a different plan: pause the memo and run a two-week space-and-tech sprint. Boost Wi-Fi capacity. Create focus pods with acoustic panels for heads-down work. Convert two corners into huddle zones with reliable hybrid kits. Post clear anchor-day norms and hybrid facilitation roles so remote people are not ghosts on a screen.

"And ultimately," she says, "if we pull off these changes, we'll make coming into the office a treat rather than a consequence."

The COO sighs, then nods. "Okay, it's a deal. We do this right. The memo waits."

Lauren smiles, thinking, *We're not anti-office. We're anti-bad office. Earn the commute, then send the memo.*

Workplace Experience

**"Ask yourself:
Why would anyone want to wake
up early, drive in bumper-to-bumper
traffic, and pay insane toll tags
and parking to work in a *less-than-
ideal* office… when they could
be more productive working
from home?"**

What it is, simplified.

Workplace Experience is how the office helps work actually happen. It is the mix of space, tech, and rituals that lets people switch between focus and collaboration without friction.

The teams that get this right know one thing: you design for peak attendance, not average. If everyone showed up on the same day, the office should still feel functional, focused, and inspiring. Every square foot should earn its keep by making work easier, faster, or more human.

Non-negotiables for a modern office space that works:
- strong, stable Wi-Fi at every seat
- desks or tables that fit real gear, including laptops, monitors, power within reach, and a spot for a backpack
- meeting rooms with one-tap join and booking systems that sync with work calendars
- ample parking and clear wayfinding from door to desk, accessible for all

- café space or nearby food options for breaks and real lunches
- phone booths or quiet rooms for calls, especially in open-plan offices
- ADA-compliant design that allows employees with mobility needs equal, safe access to the workplace

Heads-Up vs. Heads-Down work, simplified.

Here's the paradigm shift: in-office time is made for **Heads-Up** work. That includes:

- brainstorming with others
- collaboration and co-design work that is best done face-to-face
- team-building time that strengthens connection, trust, and respect
- pitching ideas to leaders
- decision-making

Everything else is **Heads-Down** work, which can often happen more easily from home or in dedicated focus areas at the office.

When you think about work in these terms, Heads-Up versus Heads-Down, you start to see the office differently. Give both modes a home. Create huddle areas with hybrid kits and focus pods with acoustic control.

Think about how an employee might move throughout the day to do their best work: from a collaboration zone for an early morning brainstorm, to the café for lunch with the team, to a focus pod for uninterrupted work. What do they need in each space to make that possible?

Measure how spaces are used. Fix the bottlenecks. Keep a short backlog of upgrades so the office improves every quarter based on what you hear in pulse surveys. When the office runs like a well-oiled machine, people are more willing, and sometimes even excited, to leave the house and come in.

Why it matters now

For most people, "RTO" - or Return to Office - triggers an eye-roll. You have to flip the script and show people why coming into the office is meaningfully better than working solo at home. Yes, for some, that is a hard sell. But when you tune the physical space and the surrounding rituals to the work, people start to see the office as a benefit.

RTO mandates without meaning drive attrition and cynicism.

The office becomes the secret ingredient that helps people do better work. It supports faster decisions, better brainstorming, and a stronger sense of belonging.

Over time, ticket noise drops, Wi-Fi, room, and AV issues decrease, meeting quality rises, and collaboration becomes the reason people come in, not a forced rule they resent.

You have to sell the commute. Show people why a day in the office beats solo work at home for this kind of work, on this day. Make the benefits obvious: decisions made, ideas shipped, and real face time. Then people choose the office because it helps them accomplish more.

Common mistakes & pitfalls (so you can avoid them)

Mistake	Solution
"Desk density = productivity"	Create experience zones in the office for different needs: Focus, Huddle, Sprint, Social, Reset. Label each area and consider naming wings or meeting rooms after the company's core values so people can remember them more easily. Post clear norms for when to use each space.
Meetings centered only on the people in the room and not on the video call	Run meetings hybrid by design. Assign a remote co-host, open a shared document, do an in-room mic and camera check, take the first question from someone remote, and capture decisions live where everyone can see them.
Anchor days with zero purpose	Publish why people are in the office that day and the outcomes they are expected to produce. Help people understand why they are meeting in person instead of commuting in just to sit on Zoom all day.

No place for quiet work → Add bookable focus nooks. Create a simple noise policy and clear Heads-Down signals so coworkers know when not to interrupt.

AV roulette, where you never know what you'll get when you book a meeting room → Standardize the kit in every room: camera, ceiling mic or table puck, screen sharing, quick-start card, and QR code for IT help. Add collaboration basics too, such as whiteboards, dry-erase markers, sticky notes, and pens. Make sure the booking system and facility map show room capacity so people can book the right space every time.

Space redesign without data → Run a light study first. Count room usage, note friction points, and survey the jobs to be done versus the space needed to do them. For example, the payroll team may need a secure area with badge access, plus a place nearby to step out and get fresh air. Spend the budget where it hurts most.

Frontline and remote-only employees ignored → If you are investing in the corporate office in a significant way, make sure these groups get an upgrade too. Give them equivalent rituals: mobile-friendly updates, shift-friendly recognition, access to workspace when needed, and travel stipends for key moments.

One simple tip — #DoTheThing (this week)

Goal: In 90 minutes, draft one team's Anchor Day Plan v1 together: what work gets done, which decisions get made, the meeting mix, the KPIs, the tests, and the space or tech upgrades needed.

Who's involved (8–12 people): HR facilitator, team lead, 1–2 individual contributors from each sub-team, one manager, one IT or Facilities representative, and one remote co-host.

Prep (10 minutes, async beforehand):

- Post a one-pager: "Why anchor days?" plus today's agenda
- Run a quick pulse with three questions:

  » What work benefits most from being in person?
  » What blocks you on-site?
  » What is one wish for the space or the tech?

Sprint agenda (90 minutes, live):

Frame (10 minutes)

Purpose: "Design how we'll use anchor days to decide faster and ship better." Show the pulse results on one slide.

Keep the working doc open on screen, and let the remote co-host drive the notes.

Define the work (15 minutes)

Brainstorm Heads-Up work, such as brainstorming, co-drafting, decision meetings, onboarding, and retros, versus Heads-Down work, such as deep focus and analysis.

Decide: anchor days are for Heads-Up work first. Heads-Down work happens only in focus blocks or quiet rooms.

Pick the three decisions (10 minutes)

Agree on three decisions the team will make on the next anchor day, for example

Q2 roadmap trade-offs, launch risks, or a final hiring slate.
Add owners and time boxes.

Meeting mix (15 minutes)

Choose formats and lengths:
- 10-minute stand-up for outcomes and blockers
- 30-minute brainstorm using a Diverge → Converge template
- 20-minute walk-and-talk 1:1s between manager and individual contributors
- 45-minute sprint block in pairs or trios to push a draft live

Set hybrid norms: remote first voice, shared doc, mic check, and live decision capture.

KPIs + tests (15 minutes)
KPIs: decision cycle time, drafts shipped, hybrid meeting score, space utilization, ticket noise from Wi-Fi, audio/video (A/V), or room issues.

Tests for the next two anchor days: a 45-minute sprint block, a no-meeting half hour for focus, remote-first facilitation, and an end-of-day five-question pulse.

Space and tech upgrades (10 minutes)
List the must-fix issues: Wi-Fi dead zones, booking systems, extra huddle kits, phone booths, wayfinding, power and HDMI access, acoustic panels.
Tag each as either:
- Quick win (14 business days or less)
- Plan (60 business days or less)

Assign owners.

Lock the plan (15 minutes)
Draft Anchor Day Plan v1 using the template below.
Confirm owners and dates.
Schedule the next anchor day and a 10-minute retro at the end.

Anchor Day Plan v1 — Template (fill in live)

Purpose: Why we meet in person and what success looks like

Three decisions to make: D1 / D2 / D3 (owner + time box)

Meeting mix: stand-up, brainstorm, 1:1s, 45-minute sprint block, social touch

Hybrid norms: remote co-host, shared doc link, first voice remote, live decision log

KPIs: pick three, such as decision cycle time, drafts shipped, hybrid score, space use %, ticket noise

Tests: two to three experiments for the next two anchor days

Space and tech upgrades: quick wins / plans with owners and ETAs

Risks and blockers: __________________

Next anchor day: date + facilitator + remote co-host

Afterward, publish a five-bullet recap:
- What we decided
- What shipped today
- Who owns what, by when
- One learning
- One tweak for next time

Reuse this template every anchor day. Keep it simple enough to repeat.

30-day workplace experience sprint

Days 1–3: Frame

Pick two pilot teams. Define the work that benefits from people being in the same place, at the same time. Name a Workplace Experience owner.

Days 4–6: Study

Walk the floor. Note used and wasted spaces, noise, Wi-Fi, power, and way-finding issues.

Run a five-question pulse:

- What helps you work well here?
- What gets in your way most often?
- Where do you struggle to focus?
- What space or tech issue slows you down?
- What is one upgrade that would make coming in feel more worth it?

Days 7–10: Quick wins

Label zones. Post room norms. Fix the top AV pain point. Add two bookable focus nooks.

Days 11–15: Anchor days

Set one weekly anchor day for each pilot. Publish the outcomes, roles, and agenda for the day. Train facilitators.

Days 16–20: Hybrid quality

Standardize meeting kits in every room: camera, microphone, screen sharing, a quick-start card, and basic collaboration tools. Add a remote co-host role.

Introduce shared docs and a two-minute recap ritual.

Two-minute recap ritual

Close every meeting with four things:
- what we decided
- who owns what
- when it is due
- what happens next

Days 21–24: Programming

Add a 30-minute demo-and-decide block where teams show work in progress, get feedback, and make one clear decision before the meeting ends. Rotate in a customer story or an internal story that shows the company's values in action.

Days 25–27: Measure

Track room utilization, meeting ratings, and time to decision, meaning how many days it takes for the team to move from discussing an issue to making a clear call with an owner and next step. Fix one friction point.

Days 28–30: Decide

Share the results. Keep, tweak, or drop each practice. Publish the next-month plan and owners.

Momentum moves (scale that works)

Experience zones: Put a simple map at the door. Show people where to Focus, Huddle, Sprint, Social, and Reset so they can move throughout the day to the zone that best supports the Heads-Up or Heads-Down work they need to do in that moment.

Anchor-day playbook: Create an outcomes template that defines the purpose, top decisions, expected deliverables, owners, prep work, and success measures for the day. Add a facilitation guide, shared doc, and recap script.

Hybrid meeting kit: Use the same gear, setup, and quick-start card in every room to create consistency.

Wayfinding + etiquette: Add clear signage, QR help, and short norms, such as "when the team is making a decision, close laptops and stay in the conversation."

Signage that reinforces values: Look for places where the company's core values and guiding principles can come to life. For example, display short "values in action" stories in shared spaces, or add simple prompts in meeting rooms that connect daily decisions back to the values.

Rethink the bathrooms: Could the back of stall doors share company news or upcoming events? Could the music shift throughout the day to feel more energizing, upbeat, or fun? It sounds silly, but even small details like this can change how a place feels.

Frontline parity: Provide mobile updates, on-site huddles, rotating leader visits, and travel support for important cross-site moments.

Office hours: Have IT and Facilities walk the floor weekly and fix issues in real time. Small things matter. If the dish sponge in the communal kitchen has not been replaced in months, people notice. The little details shape how cared for a workplace feels.

METRICS THAT MATTER

Workplace Experience Metrics	What It Tells You
Hybrid meeting satisfaction (1–5)	Quality of collaboration.
Time to decision (days)	Speed gained from anchor days.
Collaboration space utilization (%)	Whether zones are being used as intended on anchor days.
Wi-Fi / AV incident rate	The trend in tech friction.
In-office day ROI pulse ("Was today worth the commute?")	Perceived value.
Cross-site participation rate	Equity for remote teams and other sites.

Pick three to four to publish monthly. Keep them stable so you can see trend lines over time.

Using AI to simplify (Workplace Experience)

Use Case	Good Prompt	Even Better Prompt
Draft an anchor-day plan	"Create an anchor-day agenda."	"You are a workplace facilitator with 10 years experience. Draft a one-page anchor-day plan for a 12-person Product team. Include goals, roles, and a run of show for arrival, sprint, demo, decision, and social time. Add hybrid norms and a two-minute recap script. Use plain English."
Hybrid meeting checklist	"Make a hybrid checklist."	"Create a 10-step hybrid meeting checklist for rooms with a single camera and table mic. Include a pre-flight, first remote voice, shared doc link, decision capture, and backup plan if AV fails."
Space-use mini study	"Write a space survey."	"Design a one-week space-use study with a tally sheet, a five-question pulse, and an observation guide for noise, power, and wayfinding. Output printable templates."
Room norms signage	"Write room rules."	"Write three 50-word room-norms cards for a Focus Nook, Huddle Room, and Sprint Space. Include purpose, etiquette, and booking rules. Keep the tone friendly."
Post-meeting recap	"Summarize a meeting."	"Turn these notes into a six-bullet recap: decisions, owners, due dates, risks, and next demo date. Keep it under 120 words."

Quick AI guardrails reminder:

- Strip names and any personally identifiable information (PII) before pasting content into AI. This includes anything confidential, internal-only, or not meant to be shared outside your organization.
- Treat outputs as "dirty first drafts." A human should always review, proofread, and own the final wording, decisions, and recommendations.
- Use AI to speed up drafts, meeting guides, signage copy, and recap notes, not to invent workplace fixes your Facilities, IT, or leadership teams cannot actually deliver.
- Review every output for bias, accessibility issues, hallucinations, and operational gaps before anything goes live.
- Log what AI touched for transparency.

REAL·WORLD CASE STUDY

When Less Space Created More Connection

After COVID, many organizations found themselves paying for office space no one was using. One financial services firm faced this exact problem—only magnified.

Within a single city, the company operated multiple offices for the same business unit. Post-pandemic downsizing and remote work reduced in-office attendance to just 12 people occupying a massive, outdated floor. The space felt empty, inefficient, and quietly demoralizing. Leaders questioned why they were paying to keep the lights on in what had become a football-field-sized reminder of "how things used to be."

That's when **Wynter Walsh (Senior Construction Project Manager [Real Estate Services - Design and Construction])** was brought in.

The Challenge: Right-Sizing Without Breaking Trust

The mandate was clear: consolidate locations, reduce real estate costs, and design a space that would actually support hybrid work. But the risks were real. Employees were being asked to give up private offices and assigned desks. Leaders worried about morale, retention, and productivity. Budget was tight. Timelines were even tighter—one lease expiration dictated the entire project schedule.

On top of that, the organization relied on a standardized, spreadsheet-driven, one-size-fits-all design approach—treating every team as if they worked the same way. Wynter knew that assuming one solution could fit all roles would ultimately undermine the redesign in a hybrid environment.

The Strategy: Design for Behavior, Not Headcount

Instead of defaulting to desks per person, Wynter anchored the redesign on one principle: people move through different modes of work throughout the day—and the space should support that movement.

The team began with "bubble diagrams," mapping zones for collaboration, focus, privacy, and client engagement. High-traffic areas lived near the entrance. Quiet, heads-down spaces were intentionally placed away from noise. Focus rooms, lactation rooms, and technology-free areas created boundaries between deep work and collaboration.

Technology became a major unlock. Upgraded wireless infrastructure allowed employees to move freely without losing connectivity. Presentation spaces were elevated—not just for clients, but for internal collaboration and pride.

To address concerns about open offices, the team paired design with change management. Upgraded acoustic ceiling tiles and sound masking reduced noise. Clear signage explained how each space was intended to be used. And expectations were reinforced through communication, not enforcement.

Budget constraints forced trade-offs, fewer premium finishes, a smaller break room, but Wynter leaned heavily into transparency. Employees weren't left guessing.

She launched a simple project website with weekly construction photos, hosted open office hours for questions, and invited employees to walk the space before move-in once it was safe. On opening day, every employee received a welcome kit with practical guidance: how to connect to Wi-Fi, adjust furniture, find key amenities, and navigate the new environment.

The result? Employees felt informed, included, and invested—even when compromises were necessary.

The Outcome: From Empty Floors to Opt-In Attendance

When the space opened, it didn't transform overnight. The first two weeks were uncomfortable. People adjusted to proximity and new norms. Then something shifted.

Within weeks, attendance climbed from a handful of people to nearly 60 showing up regularly—even after the company made it clear that employees who didn't come into the office at least two days per week would be opting out of their end-of-year bonus. The redesigned space didn't deter people; it drew them in. Collaboration increased. Teams lingered to talk. Leaders noticed energy, engagement, and pride. Employees began choosing the office— not because they had to, but because it helped them do their best work.

As Wynter put it, the space became a family instead of a collection of silos.

Practical Lessons for HR & People Leaders

- Design for how people work—not how many people you have.
  Observe behaviors first. Headcount alone won't tell you what spaces you actually need.
- Pair physical redesign with change management.
  New spaces fail when employees aren't taught how to use them.
  Signage, communication, and grace periods matter.
- Over-communicate every step of the way.
  Transparency builds trust—even when budgets shrink
  or plans change.

- Give the space 90 days before making major changes.
  New environments come with discomfort. Employees need time to learn new patterns, adjust to proximity, and experiment with how different zones support their work. Wynter intentionally encouraged leaders to let teams *live in the space* for 90 days—then gather feedback and make small, informed refinements based on real usage, not first reactions.

In the end, the project proved a powerful truth: workplace experience isn't about square footage. It's about creating environments that make people want to show up and do their best work once they're there.

The 7-minute reality check
(Workplace Experience)

Set a timer for seven minutes and see what ideas come up.

1. **What work truly benefits from being together, face-to-face? Name three examples for one specific team.**

2. **Which space hurts productivity most right now? What is the first fix?**

3. **How will remote teammates have an equal voice in your next hybrid meeting?**

4. **What would make one anchor day feel worth the commute next week?**

5. **How could you surprise and delight employees in small ways that make the office feel more inviting?**

6. **What metric will you publish next month to show progress?**

**JOT DOWN
YOUR IDEAS
HERE**

**FIND
BONUS
RESOURCES
HERE**

Choose-your-own-adventure

- Want a pep talk before pitching Facilities? Head to page 295.
- Need a 15-minute anchor-day template you can copy? Page 296.
- Need a refresh on employee listening? Head to page 19.
- Ready to upgrade your managers? Head to the next chapter.

You've turned the office from random desks into a destination that helps teams decide faster and trust more.

Now let's level up the humans who run it: your people leaders and managers.

This next chapter shows HR professionals how to help people leaders become better coaches, mentors, and managers who equip and empower their teams to do the very best work of their lives. Remember that stat from the Introduction, that only 27% of managers are engaged at work globally?

We have our work cut out for us.

But I believe a few simple adjustments can shift that fast. Engagement can rise. Work can feel different for a lot of people. It's time. Your people need it.

Are you ready?

Let's dive in.

It's time to simplify: **The People Leader's Playbook: Integrity in Action.**

The Simplifiers Employee Experience Flywheel™

THE PEOPLE
LEADER'S
PLAYBOOK

10

The People Leader's Playbook: Integrity in Action

LEARN FROM LAUREN

The Manager Problem We Keep Calling "Culture"

Lauren stared at the listening data longer than she wanted to admit.

The pattern was impossible to ignore. Different teams. Same complaints:

- *I don't get feedback.*
- *I'm unclear on expectations.*

- *My manager avoids hard conversations.*
- *I'm not sure they have my back.*

In the executive meeting later that week, one leader finally said what everyone was thinking.

"Can we stop calling this a culture issue?" he said.

"Fix the managers in the middle, or we have no choice but to lay them off."

A few people laughed nervously.

Not because it was funny.

Because it was true.

Another executive jumped in.

"They're under more pressure than ever. Bigger revenue targets. Fewer resources."

"I know," Lauren said.

"But pressure doesn't excuse poor leadership. It explains it."

That's when it clicked.

The listening data pointed to a hard truth: it wasn't just culture. It was the managers.

In short, terrible bosses make for terrible jobs.

And until they faced that reality, nothing else would stick.

So Lauren took a different approach.

She didn't roll out another leadership program or send managers to an off-site.

She built a simple People Leader Playbook for real life.

One that assumed managers were overloaded, undertrained, and still expected to outperform last year on an even tighter budget.

First, she tackled emotional intelligence without calling it that.

No buzzwords.

Just practical skills managers could use right away.

A 60-minute learning lab focused on active listening without fixing, naming challenges early, and addressing issues with honesty and transparency before they escalated.

Next, she fixed 1:1s.

Not by adding more meetings to already crammed calendars, but by giving managers a simple, repeatable structure that worked under pressure:

- celebrate wins
- identify roadblocks
- define priorities
- focus on professional growth

Managers knew what to cover.

Employees knew what to expect.

Everyone wins.

Finally, she helped managers learn how to juggle it all:

- revenue goals
- performance issues
- team trust

The whole nine.

She introduced a lightweight way to capture outcomes and examples as they happened, so feedback and reviews were grounded in evidence, not bias.

Ninety days later, the shift was obvious.

Managers felt steadier.

Employees felt clearer.

And "culture" stopped being a vague complaint and started showing up as better conversations, earlier action, and fewer problems landing in HR's lap.

Lauren didn't make managers perfect.

She made them better.

And that changed everything.

People Leader & Manager Enablement

"The manager's *real* job is simple: Remove roadblocks so people are equipped and empowered to do the very best work of their lives."

What it is, simplified.

This chapter is about upgrading everyday management.

Not adding more work.

Not turning managers into therapists.

Not rolling out another leadership model that collects dust.

We need to teach our managers how to be great leaders and true advocates for their team members.

That's it.

Everything else is noise.

This playbook outlines five repeatable weekly habits that build clarity, momentum, and trust, without extra filler or busy work:

1. set clear expectations
2. run effective 1:1 meetings
3. coach vs. mentor vs. manage on purpose
4. give actionable feedback
5. close the loop (Say → Do → Show)

When people leaders and managers do these consistently, trust and respect strengthen on both sides of the relationship. More often than not, what gets labeled a culture problem starts fixing itself. Funny how that works.

Why it matters now

Teams are leaner.
Change is constant.
Tolerance for confusion is low.

People are being asked to do more with less while navigating shifting priorities and nonstop noise. In that environment, managers are no longer just task owners. They are the filter between chaos and clarity.

Work isn't just harder. It's broken in new ways.

When managers are unclear, slow, or avoidant, the cost shows up fast:

- missed priorities
- burnout
- conflict that escalates too late
- attrition labeled as "fit" issues

Better managers create:

- clearer work
- safer teams
- faster decisions
- fewer fire drills

This is not about being nice.

It's about being effective.

And right now, effectiveness depends on integrity in action:

What you say = what you do.

And whether your people trust the space between the two.

Common mistakes & pitfalls (so you can avoid them)

These mistakes are common because managers are busy, not bad. Most were promoted for strong individual performance, not trained to lead people through ambiguity and pressure.

The good news is that these fixes are simple because they work. They create clarity fast and reduce friction before problems escalate.

Mistake	**Solution**
Vague expectations are set for direct reports →	Define what good looks like, and by when.
1:1 meetings happen without any structure →	Use a simple, repeatable agenda every time. Confirm who drives the meeting, and make sure both people follow the same formula.
Managers blur coaching, mentoring, and managing, and use the wrong approach at the wrong time →	Before the conversation, decide one thing: is this about Now, Next, or Immediate? Coach for Now when performance, clarity, or delivery needs to improve. Focus on the work in front of them. Be specific. Guide the how. Mentor for Next when the conversation is about growth, career direction, or longer-term capability. Zoom out. Share perspective. Ask bigger questions. Manage for Immediate when urgent action is needed. Assign the task. Set the deadline. Run alongside them for accountability. Then move on.

(continued)

Use the SBI framework and keep it to two sentences. Situation: name when or where it happened. Behavior: describe what you observed. Impact: explain why it matters. Then stop talking. Example: "In yesterday's client meeting, you interrupted twice while they were explaining the issue. It made it harder to understand their concern and slowed the conversation down." Clear. Human. Hard to argue with.

Feedback comes too late or too soft →

Close the loop. Every time. That means three steps: say what you're going to do, do the thing, and show that it's done. Sometimes "show" is a follow-up message. Sometimes it's a decision made. Sometimes it's explaining why the plan changed. Silence breaks trust. Updates build it.

No follow-through →

One simple tip — #DoTheThing (this week)

Before your managers run their next 1:1, give them one question to anchor the conversation:

What does success look like for this person in the next two weeks?

Ask managers to do four things before the meeting:

- write it down
- say it out loud in the 1:1
- ask the employee to reflect it back
  (Is it possible? Is it realistic? What do they need to succeed?)
- confirm alignment

Then add one more step:

Schedule the check-in.

Before the meeting ends, the manager and direct report agree on when they will come back to review progress.

Two weeks later, same question. New data.

At the check-in, the manager asks:

- Did we hit the mark?
- What moved forward?
- What got in the way?
- Do we double down or pivot?
- What do you need more or less of from me to succeed?

That's it.

No new training.

No new tool.

No rollout required.

This small loop creates accountability without pressure. Expectations are clear. Progress is visible. Adjustments happen early, not after frustration sets in.

Clarity is integrity in action. Every time.

30-day manager enablement sprint

Before you start (Week 0): Choose your pilot

Pick one team or department to test this playbook first.
Look for:
- managers with direct reports
- real work pressure, not a "safe" team
- a leader willing to try new habits and give honest feedback

Start small on purpose. This is a quiet pilot to test what works and refine what doesn't.

Week 1: Create clarity in 1:1s

Introduce a standard 1:1 agenda, such as:
- wins worth celebrating
- top priorities for the week
- roadblocks the manager can help remove
- what the employee needs more or less of from their manager
- expectations for current priorities or curveballs that may shift everyone's focus

Week 2: Choose the right leadership move

Practice coaching, mentoring, or managing in real conversations.

Remember:

- **Coaching** = help the employee talk through the challenge and guide them toward potential solutions on their own
- **Mentoring** = help the employee by sharing specific advice from your own experience
- **Managing** = run alongside the employee to provide the accountability needed to get the task done

Ask before each discussion: Now, Next, or Immediate?

Week 3: Normalize usable feedback

Give one piece of SBI feedback to each direct report.
Keep it short, specific, and timely.

Week 4: Reduce surprises

Build a one-page evidence pack for each person.
Capture outcomes, examples, and observable signals.
No rollout.
No announcement.
Just start.

Momentum moves (scale with simplicity)

Train managers in 60-minute skills labs, not day-long workshops. Make the learning bite-sized and easy to implement.

Mic drop. Full stop.

Standardize tools, not personalities, so expectations stay consistent while leadership styles stay human.

Every people leader brings a different personality, tone, and presence. That is a good thing. You do not want leaders to sound the same.

What should stay consistent are the tools they use. When every manager runs 1:1s with the same structure, gives feedback using the same framework, and anchors decisions in the same evidence, work feels fair and predictable, even when leadership styles differ.

Consistency comes from shared tools, not scripted behavior.

Reinforce habits in team meetings and skip-levels.

Senior leaders should use the same tools to model what good looks like and reinforce expectations with their managers.

Make good management visible and repeatable.

Celebrate publicly when managers do it well. Course-correct privately when more support or training is needed.

Scaling leadership does not require more content or more training modules to wade through.

Keep it simple to follow.

Simple to apply.

Simple enough to fit into already full calendars.

METRICS THAT MATTER

The People Leader's Playbook Metrics	What It Tells You
1:1 completion rate	Whether managers are consistently holding the core conversations that create clarity, support, and accountability.
"I know what's expected of me" score	Whether employees feel clear on priorities, standards, and what success looks like.
Employee Relations (ER) escalations by team	Where manager issues may be lingering too long, escalating too late, or creating unnecessary friction.
Time to address performance issues	How quickly managers are identifying and addressing problems before they grow.
Voluntary attrition by manager	Whether people are choosing to stay or leave based on the quality of leadership they experience day to day.

If it doesn't move these metrics, it's not working.

Using AI to simplify (The People Leader's Playbook)

Let AI do the busywork. Keep the judgment human.

Use Case	Good Prompt	Even Better Prompt
Prepare for a fair, evidence-based performance conversation	"Help me summarize this employee's performance over the last quarter."	"Using the notes below, draft a one-page evidence summary with outcomes, specific examples, and observable signals. Keep it neutral, factual, without bias, and review-ready."
Clarify expectations before a 1:1	"Help me define expectations for this employee."	"Based on the goals below, help me define what success looks like for the next two weeks. Keep it clear, measurable, and realistic for an effective and empowering 1:1 conversation."
Choose the right leadership approach (coach vs. mentor vs. manage)	"How should I handle this employee situation?"	"Based on the situation below, tell me whether this is a coaching (Now), mentoring (Next), or managing (Immediate) conversation, and explain why. Then suggest how to open the conversation in an approachable way."
Draft clear SBI feedback	"Help me give feedback to an employee."	"Using the SBI framework, help me draft two sentences of feedback based on the situation below. Keep it specific, neutral, and focused on impact."

Improve 1:1 meeting quality	"Help me prepare for a 1:1 meeting."	"Help me prepare a focused 1:1 agenda making sure we celebrate the wins, discuss the roadblocks, reiterate our priorities, and focus on their professional growth. Include two to three questions I should ask based on the context below."
Close the loop after a commitment	"Help me follow up after a conversation."	"Draft a short follow-up message that closes the loop on what we discussed, what action was taken, and what happens next. Keep it clear and human."
Coach a manager, not do the work for them	"What should I tell this manager to do?"	"Help me draft three coaching questions I can ask this manager to help them think through the issue and decide next steps on their own."

Quick AI guardrails reminder:

- Strip names and any personally identifiable information (PII) before pasting content into AI. This includes anything confidential, sensitive, or not meant to be shared outside your organization.
- Treat outputs as "dirty first drafts." A human should always review, proofread, and own the final wording, decisions, and recommendations.
- Use AI to speed up prep work, drafts, and structure, not to replace judgment in people decisions, feedback, or performance conversations.
- Review every output for bias, hallucinations, tone issues, and factual errors before you use it with a manager or employee.
- Log what AI touched for transparency.
- Remember, AI is a tool. Integrity is a choice.

REAL-WORLD CASE STUDY

Integrity in Action Starts With Managers

When employees talk about "culture," they are often pointing to something far more specific: their manager.

Claude Silver, the world's first Chief Heart Officer at VaynerX and author of the USA Today Bestseller *Be Yourself at Work: The Groundbreaking Power of Showing Up, Standing Out, and Leading from the Heart,* has seen this pattern repeatedly. People don't leave jobs. They leave managers who avoid hard conversations, set unclear expectations, or outsource basic people leadership to HR.

The real issue is not a lack of values or engagement programs. It's that many managers were never taught how to lead through discomfort.

The Challenge: Managers Without a Playbook

In fast-moving organizations under pressure to perform, managers are often promoted for technical excellence, not people leadership skills. The result is inconsistent 1:1s, feedback that comes too late or too softly, and employees carrying emotional weight that never gets addressed.

Claude describes this as the moment when people "put on armor" at work. They protect themselves because leadership feels unpredictable or unsafe. Over time, that heaviness shows up as disengagement, conflict escalation, and turnover, often landing in Employee Relations long after the issue could have been handled directly.

The Strategy: Leading With Heart and Backbone

Claude reframes leadership as a daily practice rooted in emotional fluency, especially when giving tough feedback or leading change. She teaches managers to apply three emotional pillars: optimism, bravery, and efficiency.

Optimism is the belief that people can grow, even when performance needs to change. Bravery is having the hard conversation early, instead of avoiding it. Efficiency keeps feedback clear and focused, so it helps rather than overwhelms.

Together, these pillars allow managers to lead with integrity. Not by being overly nice or overly harsh, but by being clear, human, and consistent.

The Outcome: Trust, Clarity, and Fewer Fire Drills

When managers lead with optimism, bravery, and efficiency, teams move faster. Feedback lands without defensiveness. Employees raise issues earlier, before they escalate.

Claude has seen organizations reduce conflict, improve retention, and unlock creativity simply by upgrading everyday management habits. When leaders create clarity and follow through on what they say, people stop wasting energy protecting themselves and start putting it into their work.

Practical Lessons for HR & People Leaders

- Hard feedback works best when it's optimistic, brave, and efficient.
- Integrity is built through consistency, not intention.
- Stronger managers reduce the need for HR intervention.

This is what integrity in action looks like. Not perfection, but presence, clarity, and follow-through.

The 7-minute reality check
(The People Leader's Playbook)

Set a timer for seven minutes and journal your first honest thoughts to the questions below—no overthinking, just what's true right now.

1. **Where are managers unclear about expectations of them as people leaders right now?**
2. **Which manager conversations am I avoiding because they feel uncomfortable or messy?**
3. **Where are managers blurring the lines between coaching, mentoring, and managing, and do they actually know when to use each?**
4. **What evidence do I already have that shows where we could coach managers more effectively?**
5. **What patterns am I seeing in our Employee Relations insights that could help me connect the dots?**
6. **Where do I need to close the loop with a manager this week to reinforce follow-through?**

Answer honestly.
Then take one small step that helps your managers lead better.

JOT DOWN
YOUR IDEAS
HERE

FIND
BONUS
RESOURCES
HERE

Choose-your-own-adventure

- Need a breathing exercise to get centered and clear?
  Head to page 299.
- Need a change of pace and want to listen to a podcast episode
  on being a better people leader? Head to page 300.
- Need a refresh on employee listening? Head to page 19.
- Ready to learn how to report progress to senior leadership
  on all your EX efforts so far? Head to the next chapter.

You've just upgraded how managers show up day to day.
Clearer expectations. Earlier conversations. Fewer surprises.
That is the foundation.

Now comes the part that gets measured.

Because better managers do not just improve morale.
They improve decision-making.
Consistency.
Trust.
Respect.
That creates a ripple effect: stronger customer experience.
And ultimately, revenue.
The next chapter shifts the conversation from doing the right things to proving they work. You'll learn how to treat culture as a competitive advantage, not a vibe, using scorecards, EX → CX line of sight, and executive-ready stories that earn continued investment.

When culture is clear, measurable, and reinforced consistently, it becomes a true business advantage.

Are you ready?
Let's dive in.
It's time to simplify: **Culture as a Competitive Advantage.**

The Simplifiers Employee Experience Flywheel™

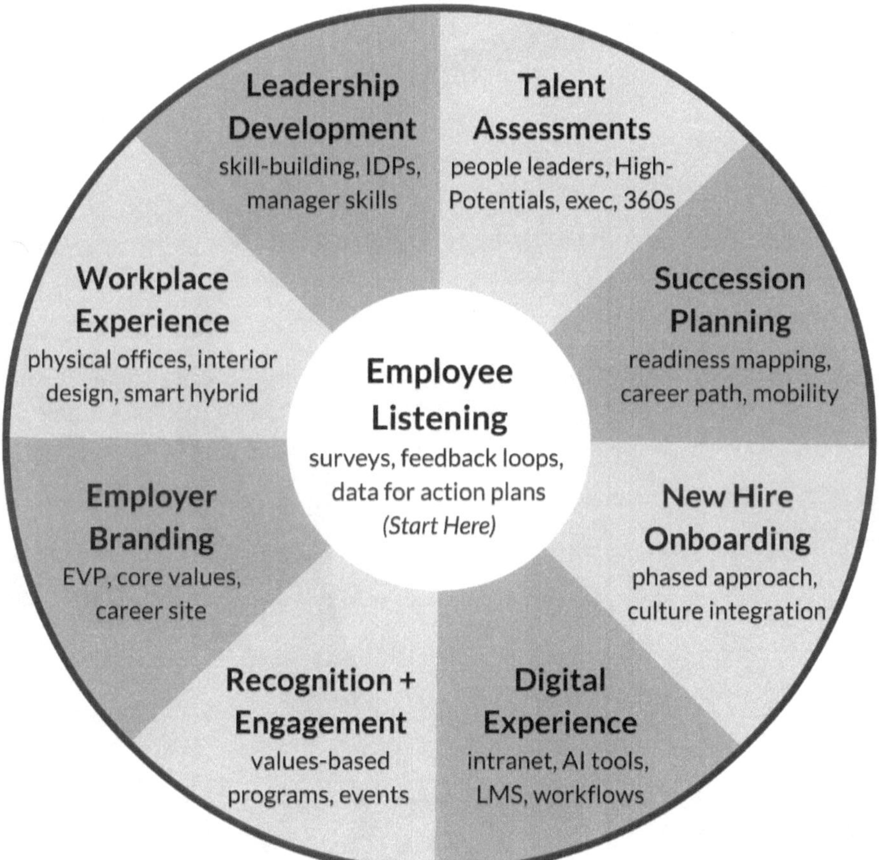

Leadership Development
skill-building, IDPs, manager skills

Talent Assessments
people leaders, High-Potentials, exec, 360s

Workplace Experience
physical offices, interior design, smart hybrid

Succession Planning
readiness mapping, career path, mobility

Employee Listening
surveys, feedback loops, data for action plans
(Start Here)

Employer Branding
EVP, core values, career site

New Hire Onboarding
phased approach, culture integration

Recognition + Engagement
values-based programs, events

Digital Experience
intranet, AI tools, LMS, workflows

CULTURE AS A
COMPETITIVE
ADVANTAGE

11

Better EX = Better CX = Better Business Results: Culture as a Competitive Advantage

"What employees experience every day will always shape culture more than what leaders say they value."

—Mary

True ROI, not vibes

Lauren walks into the executive review with two slides and a quiet confidence.

The CFO squints. "So... how's culture?"

Lauren smiles. "Thriving. I brought proof."

The COO leans in. "Please don't say 'the vibe is improving.'"

"I would never," Lauren says. "In fact, here's what changed, what it cost, what we got back, and what we're doing next."

She starts with a mindset shift: culture is not a poster. It is a growth engine. And the executive leadership team is starting to realize that HR is not just a cost center. It can be a profit center for the business. It attracts talent, keeps top performers, and protects customer promises when the business gets messy.

So she builds a simple culture scorecard. Not a 47-metric book report that no one will read. Just a concise, compelling scorecard with a few signals that matter. She ties two employee experience metrics to leadership goals, clearly showing that better employee experience leads to better customer experience and stronger business results.

Then she shows the business result: fewer escalations, steadier service, and higher customer satisfaction.

The CEO nods and cracks a small smile. "Keep going."

Lauren leaves the room with a budget to scale. Not because she made culture sound nice. Because she made it measurable.

Culture as a Competitive Advantage

"Your human capital is your greatest asset. Not your products and services. Not your customer lists. Not your vendors. Your people. They innovate, improve margins, and turn customers into loyal fans. Smart companies treat culture like a growth engine - not an afterthought."

What it is, simplified.

Culture is the pattern of how work really gets done. It is what people do when no one is watching and, equally, what leaders should reward and celebrate when everyone is watching.

Culture as a competitive advantage means this: you design the employee experience on purpose so customers feel the positive effect. When employees have clarity, tools, and trust, they are equipped and empowered to do great work. Customer service becomes more consistent and improves over time because your people are plugged in, engaged in their work, and always looking for ways to innovate.

Consistency builds customer loyalty. Loyalty grows revenue.

When you embrace this mindset, your job is to show the executive leadership team the results in a succinct and compelling way, backed by data.

In this chapter, I'm going to show you how to do exactly that: How to connect employee signals to customer outcomes, then show the receipts.

Why it matters now

Budgets are tighter and patience is shorter. Leaders still want growth, but they also want proof.

If you cannot connect your EX culture work to actual business results, did it make us money or save us money, culture gets labeled as optional or dismissed as fluff.

And that is a mistake.

Culture drives execution.

Execution drives customer experience.

Customer experience drives repeat business, referrals, and profit.

Better EX →
Better CX →
Better Business Results.

Customers are less forgiving now too. One bad handoff, one slow response, or one burned-out team member, and your brand pays for it.

This is why the EX → CX line of sight matters so much. It turns culture from "sort of important" into "non-negotiable and funded."

Common mistakes & pitfalls (so you can avoid them)

Mistake	Solution
Measuring everything, owning nothing	If your dashboard has 47 metrics, it means nothing, and no one is reading it. Time to simplify. Pick 5–8 focused metrics that reflect employee experience and show how each ties back to business results. Name an owner for each one and set a standard review cadence.
Leading with lag metrics only, like attrition, revenue, Net Promoter Score (NPS), or sick days	Add lead indicators too, like clarity, manager behaviors, time to answer, and workload. Lag metrics tell you what happened after things already went sideways. Lead indicators tell you what is happening before those outcomes show up. If you only watch lag metrics, you are driving by looking in the rearview mirror. Keep your eyes on the road and your hands on the EX Flywheel.
Vanity numbers, high participation but no change	Pair every metric with a decision: *If this moves, what will we do?* Name the owner and the trigger, so it does not become interesting data with no action attached. Example: "If role clarity drops below 75% favorable, we run a two-week clarity sprint, managers reset priorities, publish the top three outcomes, and we re-pulse in 14 days."

Publish: **You Said / We Did / Here's What's Next**
with names and dates. Make it visible
in the places people already use, like Slack,
the intranet, or all-hands updates, and keep
it short enough to scan in 30 seconds.
If you cannot act yet, say so plainly and name
what would need to change to revisit it.

Data without a close-the-loop plan

Truth is, culture is everyone's job.
Tie one or two EX metrics to leadership goals
so culture stops being "an HR initiative"
and becomes "how we run the business." Pick
metrics leaders can actually influence, like
manager 1:1 cadence, time to answer
on top employee tasks, or team clarity scores.
Then pair those with two or three required actions
leaders must own. HR runs the system. Leaders
own the outcomes.

Treating culture like HR's job

Numbers alone do not win you the budget. Stories
do. Use a simple three-part narrative every time:
Problem → Action → Result. But first, lead with
the recommendation. Start with one clear
sentence that says what you want leaders
to do next. That grabs attention fast. Then name
the human pain in one sentence to make it real.
From there, show what changed and what moved.
Seal it with one customer example that makes
the link undeniable. One crisp story turns your
dashboard into a decision.

A scorecard with no story

If your culture scorecard only reflects
HQ and desk-based employees,
you are measuring only one part of the company.
Frontline teams live in shifts, sites, and systems
that they do not control. Build the scorecard with
frontline input and frontline constraints in mind.
Then fix what is broken, from faulty equipment
to unclear handoffs to slow approvals. If it does
not work for the people closest to the customer,
it is not culture. It is just talk.

Ignoring frontline reality

One simple tip — #DoTheThing (this week)

Pick one customer promise you care about: speed, quality, warmth, or trust.

In 45 minutes, map it like this:

- **Employee signal (lead):** What must be true internally?
- **Behavior:** What do we want people to do consistently? Can we tie it to one of our company's core values or guiding principles?
- **Customer result (lag):** What should customers notice?

Then choose one metric for each line and put it on one page.

That is your first culture scorecard.

30-day culture as a competitive advantage sprint

Goal: Prove one clear EX → CX win in 30 business days, then show the results to your executive leadership team so you can expand and scale.

Days 1–3: Pick the line of sight

Choose one customer promise, for example: *fast, accurate support.*

Pick two employee signals that drive it, for example: tool friction and role clarity.

Pick one customer metric to track, such as Customer Satisfaction Score (CSAT) or first-response time, to see whether customers actually feel the improvement.

Days 4–6: Baseline and focus

Pull the baseline for the three metrics.

Run five quick employee interviews across roles and shifts, 15 minutes each.

Identify the top two friction points slowing good work down.

Days 7–12: Ship two fixes

Fix #1: remove one obvious blocker, such as access, a broken process, or an unclear handoff.

Fix #2: standardize one "how we work" behavior, such as escalation rules in plain English.

Create one simple page where the new process lives.

Days 13–18: Enable leaders

Give managers a five-sentence script explaining what changed, why it matters, and what to do now.

Add one leader habit, for example: a weekly 10-minute blockers sweep.

Track adoption lightly with a checklist, not bureaucracy.

Days 19–23: Close the loop

Publish You Said / We Did / Here's What's Next with names and dates.

Share one short customer quote or frontline story that shows the impact.

Days 24–30: Prove and pitch

Re-measure the three metrics.

Lead with one concise recommendation, what you want the executives to do next, then walk them through a five-slide update:

Baseline → Action → Result → Next Bet → Ask.

Secure the next 30-day sprint and expand to the next team.

Momentum moves

Culture scorecard cadence: Set a regular monthly pulse and a quarterly reset. Stay consistent and track the same metrics over time so the trend lines mean something.

One executive sponsor: Identify and secure someone who will remove roadblocks for <u>you</u>, not just cheer you on from the sidelines. You need an advocate in the room. You need an advocate in the room who champions your EX work.

Two leader habits: Pick two behaviors you want leaders to repeat weekly, like clarity, recognition, or blocker removal, and roll out simple training so they can do them consistently.

One "how we win" playbook: Create a short one-pager that defines the key behaviors customers should feel. Clearly define what a world-class customer experience looks like at your organization.

A visible backlog: Keep a simple, shared list of open employee experience fixes and improvements, with the theme, owner, status, and ETA for each item. Keep it public so trust stays alive.

Celebrate wins with proof: People can see right through hype. Use the data and tell the truth. "We reduced time to answer by 32% over the last six months" lands much better than a vague claim ever will.

METRICS THAT MATTER

Culture as a Competitive Advantage Metrics	What It Tells You
Role clarity (Top-2 box*)	Whether people know what good looks like and how they win.
Tool friction or time to answer ("How do I...?")	How much work time is being wasted on finding the basics.
Manager 1:1 cadence (self-report or calendar proxy)	Whether leaders are doing the weekly work of leadership, and whether you can catch the gaps early.
Workload sustainability (Top-2 box)	Whether people are being burned out just to hit unrealistic goals.
Ticket volume by type (IT / People Ops)	Where the system is breaking and creating noise or overwhelm.
Customer CSAT or Net Promoter Score (NPS) for the targeted journey	Whether the customer actually felt the improvement.
Regretted attrition in key roles or your high-potential (HiPo) population	Whether you are keeping the talent you cannot easily replace.

*Top-2 box = Agree + Strongly Agree combined in your listening survey.

Pick five to seven metrics and publish them every quarter. Use the same set and show the trends. That is what helps your executive leadership team make better decisions as you pitch scaling your EX strategy over time.

Always connect the dots: this EX initiative helped employees deliver a better customer experience, which supported revenue growth, customer retention, and stronger business results.

That is the secret sauce of this entire book.

Using AI to simplify (Culture as a Competitive Advantage)

Use Case	Good Prompt	Even Better Prompt
Build an EX → CX map	"Map employee experience to customer experience."	"You are an Employee Experience (EX) strategist with 10 years experience. Create an EX → CX (Customer Experience) line-of-sight map for this customer promise: [promise]. Output a table with employee signal (lead), leader behavior, operational proof, customer metric (lag), and the simplest way to measure each."
Draft a culture scorecard	"Make a culture dashboard."	"Create a one-page culture scorecard for a _____-person hybrid company. Include 5–7 metrics split into lead and lag. For each metric, include the definition, owner, cadence, and what decision we make if it moves. Map it as an editable table to serve as a scorecard."
Write the executive story	"Write an exec update about culture."	"Write a five-slide narrative for senior leaders: Lead with the recommendation first (as concise as possible, what I want them to do next), then go into the problem, why it matters, what we changed, results with numbers, next bet, and the budget ask. Tone: direct and professional. Help me identify one short and compelling frontline story from our organization that drives this narrative. Do not make anything up."

Create a quarterly operating rhythm	"Create a governance plan."	"Design a lightweight operating rhythm for culture work: monthly check-in agenda (30 minutes), quarterly review agenda (60 minutes), roles (executive sponsor, HR owner, operations partner), and what gets published after each."
Bias and clarity check	"Edit for clarity."	"Act as a clarity and bias checker. 1) Rewrite in plain English. 2) Flag vague claims and ask for proof. 3) Remove biased phrasing. Return the revised version plus a short list of flags."

Quick AI guardrails reminder:

- Strip names and any personally identifiable information (PII) before pasting content into AI. This includes anything confidential, sensitive, or not meant to be shared outside your organization.
- Treat outputs as "dirty first drafts." A human should always review, proofread, and own the final wording, decisions, and recommendations.
- Use AI to speed up scorecards, summaries, and draft narratives, not to invent results, promises, or business claims you cannot prove.
- Review every output for bias, hallucinations, weak logic, and vague claims before you put it in front of leaders.
- Log what AI touched for transparency.

REAL-WORLD CASE STUDY

One Company, One Language: Turning Culture Into a Business Advantage at Jack Henry

The real test of culture is not what leaders say. It is how consistently employees show up for each other and for customers.

At Jack Henry, a financial technology company, **Chief People Officer Holly Novak** and the leadership team set out to create that consistency across a rapidly growing organization.

The Challenge: Too Many Principles, Not Enough Consistency

Jack Henry had a strong culture, but after decades of acquisition-driven growth and a highly dispersed workforce, consistency became harder to maintain.

Over the company's 50-year history, more than 40 acquisitions brought together different teams, systems, and leadership styles. Along the way, the company accumulated values, leadership frameworks, and guiding principles that made sense individually but created confusion when combined.

Leaders and employees struggled to answer a simple question: What does great leadership actually look like here?

Without a shared language, some business units began creating their own frameworks. That fragmentation risked inconsistent employee experiences and, over time, could lead to inconsistent customer experiences.

At the same time, Jack Henry was undergoing a major, multi-year transformation called One Jack Henry, designed to unify the organization. Novak and her team recognized that without alignment around a clear way of leading and serving clients, continued growth would only amplify those inconsistencies.

The Strategy: Creating "The Jack Henry Way"

The solution was to simplify.

Novak's team developed The Jack Henry Way, a framework defining how leaders operate across the organization. It centers on three pillars:

- People
- Service
- Results

At the center sits the One Jack Henry mindset, reinforcing that every employee contributes to the same purpose regardless of role or department.

The transformation began with defining the company's first formal purpose statement, helping employees connect their daily work to the success of banks and credit unions. From there, the organization aligned several initiatives around that foundation, including a refreshed talent value proposition, a dedicated Employee Experience team, and leadership development reaching more than 2,200 leaders.

Leaders helped shape the framework as well. Service leaders defined the behaviors required to deliver consistent client experiences, creating ownership across the organization.

As Novak explains, "Culture cannot be owned by HR alone. HR supports the work, but the leadership team must champion it."

The Outcome: Stronger Alignment, Stronger Engagement

Several signals showed the culture shift taking hold.

Jack Henry moved from an annual engagement survey to a continuous feedback strategy throughout the year. Participation climbed to 87 percent, up from historical levels below 60 percent. For Novak, that level of response signals trust because employees feel safe sharing feedback.

The transformation also changed how teams serve customers. In the past, employees might redirect clients to another business unit. Today, the expectation is different.

The philosophy is simple: "I can take care of that."

Instead of passing customers across departments, employees take ownership of finding the answer.

Internally, collaboration improved as leaders began operating as one company rather than separate divisions. As alignment increased internally, service consistency improved for clients as well, reinforcing the link between employee experience and customer experience.

The impact also shows up in retention. Across more than 7,300 employees, Jack Henry's average tenure is 10.4 years, reflecting a culture where people choose to stay and grow.

Practical Lessons for HR & People Leaders

- Simplify the cultural message. Too many frameworks create confusion. Define a clear way leaders are expected to lead and serve.
- Track the signals that matter. Engagement, trust, and belonging provide early indicators of whether culture is strengthening or weakening.
- Make leadership responsible for culture. HR can design the framework, but leaders must actively champion it.

Culture becomes a competitive advantage when it is clear, measurable, and reinforced consistently across the organization.

The 7-minute reality check

(Culture as a Competitive Advantage)

Set a timer for seven minutes. Answer fast.

1. **What customer promise matters most this quarter?**
2. **What is the one internal friction point that makes that promise harder to deliver?**
3. **What leader behavior or EX resource would remove that friction the fastest?**
4. **What metric will prove progress in the next 30 business days?**
5. **If this improves, what will you scale next?**

Choose-your-own-adventure

- Need help turning culture into a five-slide executive pitch?
  Head to page 301.
- Want a one-page scorecard you can copy today? Head to page 303.
- Need a quick reset before you open another dashboard tab?
  Head to page 299.
- Need a refresh on employee listening? Head to page 19.
- Ready to finish this book? Head to the next chapter.

Perfection is not the aim here.

You need a clean line of sight, a few metrics to track, and proof you can put in front of decision-makers with confidence. When you can show that a better employee experience drives a better customer experience, culture stops being a nice-to-have.

EX work becomes strategy.

Now comes the fun part: turning all of this into a simple, repeatable rhythm you can run starting next Monday.

One page.
A few numbers.

One story.
Owners, dates, and a clear what we're doing next.

Are you ready?
Let's dive in.
It's time to simplify: **The Conclusion — Your Action Plan for Next Monday.**

The Simplifiers Employee Experience Flywheel™

YOUR ACTION
PLAN FOR
NEXT MONDAY

Your Action Plan for Next Monday

"Better employee experience does not happen through grand gestures. It happens through simple actions done consistently over time."

—Mary

LEARN FROM LAUREN

Hands on the wheel, let's go.

Thirty days in, Lauren walks into the executive meeting calm, cool, collected, and confident, with one page in her hand. No deck. No speech. No vibes. Just proof, and pride in everything she has been able to move so far.

"Here's what changed," she says, sliding the scorecard across the table.

"Meeting time is down 14%. 'How do I...?' time to answer is down 41%. And 'When I speak up, someone follows up' is up 9 points."

The CFO squints. "Cost?"

Lauren doesn't flinch. "Two weeks of focused work. A shared agenda template. One intranet update. Net result: more time for billable work."

The COO leans back and nods. The CHRO smiles like, finally.

Someone from Operations asks, "So, what now?"

Lauren points to the bottom of the page. "I'm glad you asked. I say we scale the pilots next in Product and Customer Operations. Each gets a named owner, a 30-day target, and a visible communication cadence: You Said / We Did / Here's What's Next. We're building momentum. People are seeing the difference. We're headed in the right direction."

She adds one more line. "And I highly recommend we do a manager refresh too, reinforcing five habits of strong people leadership: setting clear expectations, running crisp 1:1s, giving usable feedback, knowing when to coach versus mentor, and closing the loop."

A frontline leader speaks up from the back of the room. "I couldn't agree more. This stuff is actually working. For the first time, I can tell my team what is changing, who owns it, and when. That steadies people, and they're showing up differently at work. I can verify, it's definitely working."

The COO nods again. "Excellent. Keep going. Same time next month. Bring me three metrics and one story."

Lauren smiles. "Deal."

Hands on the wheel, let's go.

Your Action Plan: The Simplifiers Employee Experience Flywheel

"This is your Monday plan. Not your 'someday' plan."

What it is, simplified.

The Flywheel runs in two speeds: **monthly** and **quarterly**. The first is for proof. The second is for power.

Monthly

Every 30 days, you ship one visible improvement, a quick win, and close the loop by telling your people what changed.

Small.

Clear.

Finished.

That's how you build momentum without burning people out or giving them whiplash from constant change. The energy should feel more like, *Wow, thanks for fixing that one thing. Nice.*

Quarterly

Every quarter, you zoom out, review the trend lines, refine your EX priorities, and take action on the bigger moves that naturally take longer to build, test, implement, train, and fully land.

That's how you avoid *random acts of HR(!!!)* and build a real system that improves the employee experience on purpose.

Choose the speed that fits the work.

Some things take longer to improve, build, test, implement, train, and gain adoption.

For example, creating an online portal for retail workers to order new uniforms? Fairly simple.

Creating a whole new intranet and employee engagement platform from scratch? That will take longer.

Listen → Decide → Ship → Measure → Close the Loop

No matter which speed you use, 30-day sprint or quarterly run, these five practices matter most:

Listen (always focused, not filler)

One pulse. One roundtable. Maybe even one targeted question. You are looking for friction, not fan fiction provided by Karen from Finance. Ask and listen with intent: Where is work getting stuck? Where is trust leaking? What is broken and could be better?

Decide (one priority, one owner)

Pick one fix that will remove pain for a real group of people. Name the owner. Name the date. Keep the scope small enough to ship. Don't try to fix 80 things at once or talk ideas to death without ever taking action. Choose one thing, do it well, and follow this repeatable practice: Iterate → Test → Document → Track → Refine. Then start again on the next improvement.

Ship (visible improvement)

Make the change. Update the page. Fix the workflow. Simplify the process. Train the manager on the new habit so they can cascade it to their teams. Whatever it is, people need to feel it as an improvement in daily work for it to stick. Does it make life easier? Work faster? Is the customer experience better? If not, is it really improving the employee experience?

Measure (proof, not perfection)

Track three to four metrics that match the fix. Time saved. Fewer tickets. Higher clarity. Better follow-through. If it does not change behavior or reduce friction, it is not the right metric.

Close the loop (build trust on purpose)

Publish a short update: You Said → We Did → Here's What's Next. Include names and dates. This is where trust gets built.

Remember:

"Hands on the wheel" means you do not let the Flywheel drift back into guesswork. You do not wait for the annual survey. And you definitely do not launch five things at once.

You keep steering with small, steady cycles that compound.

And that is the point: build trust with proof.

When people can see what changed, who owns it, and what is happening next, the eye-rolls stop. They start believing you. They start trusting their senior leaders bit by bit. Then they start engaging in their work again. And that is the game-changer.

Why it matters now

Because you do not get unlimited tries with your workforce.

When people feel ignored, stuck, or tired of empty promises, they leave. Or they stay and disengage. Either way, the business pays.

The EX Flywheel works because it is focused. It gives HR teams a framework for culture work, and it helps people fall back in love with work again. How? It turns good intentions into actual decisions, owners, and target dates.

And it creates the one thing leaders cannot argue with:

Progress you can point to.

One simple tip — #DoTheThing (this week)

Create your **Three Numbers + One Story** cadence.

Pick three metrics from the list below that you can move in the next 30 days. Then pick one employee story you want to earn through that action. Whose work life gets better because of this fix? Tell me the story of Carlos in IT or Rosita in B2B Sales and how this change improves their day-to-day experience.

Then put a 30-minute monthly meeting on the calendar with your executive sponsor. Title it:

EX Scorecard: Three Numbers + One Story // Check-In Call

If it is not on the calendar, it is not real.

Show up ready to tell a compelling story about what you are doing and how it is delivering better business results.

METRICS THAT MATTER

Your Action Plan for Next Monday Metrics	What It Tells You
"When I speak up, someone follows up" (Top-2 box = Agree + Strongly Agree combined)	Trust and loop closure. This is culture in one line.
How long it takes to get answers to common "How do I...?" questions	Friction. A direct measure of how hard work feels.
Meeting time per person	Capacity per employee. More time back means more work shipped.
Manager 1:1 completion (with agenda)	Coaching health. Are leaders doing the basics and are they doing them effectively?

(continued)

New-hire Day 30 Net Promoter Score (NPS)	First-impression accuracy. Did reality match the promise?
Regretted attrition (6–12 months)	Outcome. Are you keeping the people you cannot replace easily?
Internal mobility rate	Whether your organization is creating real career pathways internally, or quietly forcing people to look elsewhere to grow.

Pick five to eight metrics. Publish three to four each month. Track the same measures consistently so the trend lines tell a real story.

Using AI to simplify (Your Action Plan for Next Monday)

Use Case	Good Prompt	Even Better Prompt
Draft a one-page EX scorecard	"Make a scorecard for employee experience."	"You are an EX lead with 10 years experience. Create a one-page scorecard with 3 lead indicators, 2 lag indicators, and a 'Three Numbers + One Story' section. Include definitions, data sources, and a place for owners and next actions. Keep it in plain English."
Turn raw feedback into themes	"Summarize these survey comments."	"Cluster these comments into 5 themes. For each theme: 1) what people are saying, 2) why it matters, 3) one quick win we could likely achieve in 14 days, 4) owner role, 5) one metric to track. Flag any sensitive data."
Draft "You Said / We Did / Here's What's Next"	"Write a close-the-loop message."	"Write a close-the-loop update for employees using this structure: You Said (3 bullets), We Did (3 bullets), Here's What's Next (2 bullets with dates and owners). Tone: honest, confident, warm, and professional."

Create manager scripts	"Write a manager script."	"Create a five-sentence manager script for a team huddle: 1) what we heard, 2) what we're changing, 3) what stays the same, 4) what I need from you, 5) when we'll review. Keep it human."
Build a 30-day sprint plan	"Make a 30-day plan."	"Build a 30-business-day EX sprint plan for improving time to answer on HR policies. Include weekly goals, owners, deliverables, and the measurement plan. Also include what resources, time, money, or headcount, may be needed to implement it. Keep it simple and realistic. Create a SWOT analysis for this sprint plan, mapping out possible strengths, weaknesses, opportunities, and threats with 2-3 solutions for addressing weaknesses and threats."

Quick AI guardrails reminder:

- Strip names and any personally identifiable information (PII) before pasting content into AI. This includes anything confidential, sensitive, or not meant to be shared outside your organization.
- Treat outputs as "dirty first drafts." A human should always review, proofread, and own the final wording, decisions, and recommendations.
- Use AI to speed up the first draft creation of scorecards, summaries, and draft narratives, not to invent results, promises, or business claims you cannot prove.
- Review every output for bias, hallucinations, weak logic, and vague claims before you put it in front of leaders.
- Log what AI touched for transparency.

The 7-minute *vision* check
(Your Action Plan for Next Monday)

Today's journaling exercise is not a reality check. *It's a vision check.* Set a timer for seven minutes and imagine a future at your organization that feels night-and-day different because of the EX work you are doing right now. Write like you are describing a before-and-after photo. Paint a vision you would be proud of.

1. **Six months from now, what is obviously better?**
2. **Finish this sentence: "Work feels better here because _______."**
3. **What do people say out loud now that they were not saying before?**

Examples:

- "I know what good looks like."
- "Stuff actually gets fixed."
- "My manager follows up."
- "I actually enjoy working here now."

4. **What is one visible ritual that proves the change is real and sticking?**

Examples:

- a Walk-n-Connect meetup at the office where employees from different departments can get their steps in and connect with someone they may not know well yet, using simple, non-work conversation starter cards
- a "How do I...?" online hub that people actually use
- a monthly Lunch-and-Learn where employees teach each other a new skill, putting a playful spin on Show-and-Tell
- a manager habit their team genuinely appreciates

5. **What are your three receipts?**

   Three numbers you would be proud to show an executive: time saved, fewer tickets, higher clarity, lower regret, or faster ramp.

6. **What is your next-Monday move?**

   Name the first 30-day cycle you will run: the focus area, the owner, and the publish date for You Said / We Did / Here's What's Next.

Choose-your-own-adventure

- Need a refresh on employee listening? Head to page 19.
- Need a quick win you can ship in 14 days? Flip back to the digital employee experience chapter on page 175.
- Need to rebuild manager trust fast? Go to The People Leader's Playbook chapter on page 217.
- Need to stop overpromising and start showing receipts? Go back to employer branding on page 53.

If you have made it this far, you officially get a gold star from me. Your dedication to improving the workplace is inspiring, and I am so glad you have this playbook in your hands to help you do it.

Always remember:

Employee Experience is not a poster. It is not a perk. It is not a one-time program you launch and forget. And it is definitely not a one-off pizza party.

The Simplifiers Employee Experience Flywheel™

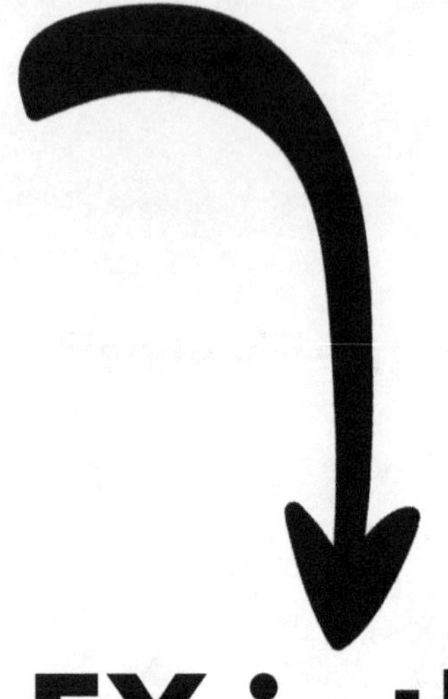

EX is the daily experience your people have of how work gets done here.

And when you improve that experience on purpose, people do not just feel better.

They do better work.

Customers feel it.

The business feels it.

The Sunday Scaries start to fade.

People sleep better. They actually like their job and look forward to tackling the work ahead of them.

You did that.

You helped make a positive impact for a lot of people. And that is no small thing.

So I hope you take a moment, hit pause, and let that truth sit with you for a second. You are making great things happen at your workplace right now. And I know how common it is, especially in HR, to keep pushing forward without much celebration or praise.

So I want to give that to you now.

The glory.

The *"Wow, I really did that!"* moment.

The realization that your work matters. Deeply.

Without you, none of this would be possible.

So if it is only my voice in your head right now, let that be enough, because I am saying:

You're doing a really great job.

Keep going.

People appreciate you more than you know.

And also, you are not behind. You are just at the beginning of the next cycle.

If you are feeling overwhelmed, let me make this simple: **you do not need a perfect plan.**

You just need a fresh start.

Pick one pain point your people feel every week. Focus on fixing the one thing that removes friction. Ship it. Measure it. Tell the truth about it. Then come back to this playbook and pick the next one thing.

Whether it is improving new hire onboarding, turning terrible bosses into trusted mentors, building recognition efforts people actually appreciate, or updating the office itself, let this playbook be your guide, with me by your side.

And if you are realizing you have zero budget, or a gaggle of cynical senior leaders who still do not buy the better EX = better CX = better business results paradigm shift, that is okay.

Do not argue.

Do not beg.

Just show the receipts by taking steady, daily, imperfect action to create proof.

Momentum builds trust.

Trust earns investment.

That is how the Flywheel turns.

Choose-your-own-adventure from here and go back to the chapter you need most. It really can be that simple.

Progress over perfection. Always.

With your hands on the wheel, you are doing the thing.

And if you have heard me say this a million times on The Simplifiers Podcast, I'm going to say it one more time:

You can do this.

I believe in you.

It's time to simplify!

Now, let's go.

SUPER PEP TALK #1

(Read this before chapter one)

Hey friend—

Before you jump into Chapter one, I want you to take a breath.

Like, a real one.

In through your nose.

Out through your mouth.

Shoulders down.

If you're feeling excited *and* a little nervous, that's not a red flag.

That's a signal.

It means you're standing at the edge of change—where growth always feels a bit wobbly before it feels strong.

You might be wondering:

- Will this playbook actually work here?
- Will people roll their eyes?
- Will senior leaders take me seriously... or label this culture work as frivolous?
- What if I try something and it falls flat?

Let's get something straight: you're not behind. You're not failing. You're *actually* right on time.

Most HR managers were never handed a simple, practical system for building trust and improving employee experience.

They were handed a never-ending to-do list and the expectation to magically "fix morale" between meetings. So if part of you feels unsure, it's **not** because you're not capable. It's because you're doing something brave: **you're choosing a brand new approach.**

Also… your ideas don't need to be perfect to be powerful.

This book isn't asking you to walk into work tomorrow and launch a sweeping culture transformation with fireworks and a 40-slide deck.

No.

We're doing this the smart way.

The Simplifiers way.

Step by step.

Test, don't guess.

Listen first.

Build proof.

Earn buy-in through results.

That's why Chapter 1 starts with Employee Listening.

Because listening isn't "soft."

It's **strategic.**

Listening gives you leverage. It gives you signal. It gives you the *right* starting point—so you're not building programs based on assumptions, leadership opinions, or whoever is loudest in the room.

And if someone calls your work "lip service," here's what you can remember:

Lip service is performative. Listening is operational.

Listening turns feelings into patterns.

Patterns into priorities.

Priorities into action.

Action into trust.

You're not chasing vibes. You're building a system.

Now, one more thing before you turn the page, friend…

Scan this QR code to listen to a quick guided visualization:

How to Ask for What You Need (guided visualization)

It's a short, calming reset to help you regulate your nervous system, steady your mind, and move forward calm, cool, collected… and confident.

You don't have to do it all today.

You just have to take the very next step.

You can do it, I believe in you.

It's time to simplify!

—Mary

SUPER PEP TALK #2

Hey friend—

First: pause.

If your brain feels like it has 37 tabs open after Chapter 1… you're not alone.

Employee listening can feel like *a lot* because it matters. You want to do it well. You don't want to mess it up. And you definitely don't want to create a big "feedback moment" that goes nowhere.

So here's your permission slip:

You do not need to implement everything you just read.

Not today. Not this week. Maybe not ever.

Right now, your job is to **simplify.**

Because when HR tries to do 20 things at once, one of two things happens:

1. nothing happens (because it's too big), or
2. you burn out trying to carry it all.

Neither is the goal.

Instead, focus on **one small listening action** you can take in the next 7 days. Then take **one small action** based on what you learn. That's how trust starts rebuilding—one solid proof point at a time.

If you only do one thing, do this:

Ask one simple question:

"If we could fix one thing in 30 days, what should it be—and why?"

That's it.

Not a 30-question pulse survey.

Not a complicated framework.

Not a six-month listening tour (unless you want one later).

Just one question that signals: *We're listening—and we intend to act.*

Then treat what you hear like a science experiment.

No ego. No defensiveness. No spiraling.

Just open curiosity.

You're not collecting feedback to be liked.

You're collecting signals to help make work better for everyone.

And yes, some feedback might sting. That doesn't mean you're failing. It means you're finally getting honest data. People are starting to trust you and your team to tell you the real truth.

The goal isn't perfect sentiment. The goal is progress.

So, here's the simple loop:

1. **Listen**
2. **Choose 1–2 priorities**
3. **Take action in 30 days**
4. **Close the loop** *("Here's what we heard. Here's what we're doing.")*
5. **Track 1–2 KPIs** (keep it simple: participation rate + one outcome metric tied to the issue)

That's how you build credibility fast.

Not with a flashy program.

With follow-through.

Now, if your nervous system is buzzing and you feel that "what if I do this wrong?" energy…

Scan this QR code to listen to:

How to Calm Your Anxiety
(guided visualization)

It'll help you breathe, settle your body, and step back into this work calm, clear, and confident.

You don't need to solve everything.
    You just need to start—small, simple, and steady.
    You've got this.

—Mary

SUPER PEP TALK #3

Hey friend—if your head is spinning right now, that makes sense. Employer branding can spark *so many* ideas at once. But you don't need a full rebrand to make real progress.

Here's the move: **pick one small truth to amplify.**

Ask yourself:

What's already good on the inside that we're not saying out loud yet?

Start there. One story. One proof point. One simple message you can repeat.

And if your brain feels noisy? Go do a quick reset. If it's sunny, **step outside for a 10–15 minute walk,** no podcast, no email, just fresh air and a little movement. Let your nervous system catch up to your ambition.

You're not behind. You're building clarity.

One honest step at a time.

PS> Did I mention yet how proud I am of you? Because, I am. You're doing great! Keep going.

—Mary

SUPER PEP TALK #4

Hey friend—I'm gonna make this short and sweet.

Look at you doing the thing.

Picture this: it's six months from now.

You're walking the halls at work and there's a fresh spark in the air. People are eating lunch together again. They're laughing. The energy feels lighter. And you can *see* the impact of the work you've been putting in—because it's real.

That is pretty darn cool.

And yes… it's happening because of you.

Keep going. One step at a time.

—Mary

SUPER PEP TALK #5

Hey friend—It's time for a brain break!

Squirrel away for the next 15 minutes and find somewhere you can go where you won't be interrupted. Maybe a focus room? Maybe go sit in your car? Wherever you go, I want you to carve out the next 15 minutes just for replenishing your spirit.

Found your spot?

Awesome.

Let's do a guided visualization together.

Scan this QR code to listen to:

How to be a Calm, Centered People Leader
(guided visualization)

We will do a breathing exercise together and help you recalibrate your brain in a calming way. Just listen to my voice and see where that takes you. See, wasn't that a nice treat?

You can do this, I believe in you. It's time to simplify!

—Mary

SUPER PEP TALK #6

Hey friend—real talk time.

Talent assessments can feel a little intimidating… especially if you've never really done them before (or you've only seen them done in a super complicated way). That's okay. You're not behind. You're just learning a new strategic lever—and it's a powerful one.

Want to spark a new idea to get you going on this section?

Start simple:

Pick one role that matters most right now.
The one that drives results, impacts customers, or holds the team together.

Then ask three quick questions:
1. What does "great" look like in this role today?
2. Who's already close to that, and what do they need next?
3. What's the biggest gap holding the rest of the team back?

That's it. No giant framework. No fancy scorecards. Just clarity you can act on.

Keep it simple to start. You can always build from there.

One role. One insight. One next step.

You've got this!

—Mary

SUPER PEP TALK #7

Hey friend—

If you're on the verge of a teeny-tiny menty B… I get it.

Leadership development can feel like a BIG topic with a BIG price tag and a BIG "where do I even start?" vibe.

Especially if you're on a tiny HR team, wearing seventeen hats, doing the work of three people, and trying to keep the wheels on the bus. *(If that's you, raise your hand right now. Yup, I feel ya.)*

So here's the truth: you don't need a full leadership program to build better leaders. You just need one small lever you can pull this month.

Consider this. Pick one:

- One leader group (new managers, frontline leads, high-potentials)
- One skill (feedback, coaching, clarity, trust)
- One simple action you can repeat (a 15-minute tool, a monthly circle, a one-page guide)

That's it. This isn't about doing everything. It's about doing *something* consistently enough that it starts to change the way people lead.

And one more thing: if this chapter pushed you way outside your comfort zone, that's not a sign to stop. That's a sign you're growing.

Take a breath. Choose the smallest next step.

You're not behind. You're building momentum.

I'm super proud of you, keep going!

—Mary

SUPER PEP TALK #8

Hey friend—

Need a spark of positive inspiration? Here it is:

The fact that you just finished this chapter means you're already doing what most people don't do. You're choosing to lead on purpose. You're choosing to build leaders, not just manage problems.

And that matters.

Because leadership development isn't about fancy programs or big budgets.

It's about small moments that compound. It's about improving:

- one better 1:1
- one clearer expectation
- one brave conversation that ends up empowering, not disheartening
- one manager who finally feels supported

That's how culture shifts.

Not overnight. But steadily. Quietly. For real.

So pick one idea from this chapter that made you think, "Ooooh… that could work here."

Write it down.

Circle it.

Try it once this week.

You don't need permission. You don't need perfection. You just need momentum.

You're closer than you think.

—Mary

SUPER PEP TALK #9

Hey friend—

Succession planning can make your brain feel like it just ran a marathon. So before you barrel into the next thing on your plate, let's take a quick reset.

Seriously. Get up from your desk.

If it's sunny, step outside for a **10-minute walk**. Let your eyes land on something that isn't a screen. Feel your shoulders drop. Breathe like you mean it.

If going outside isn't an option, make a **hot drink** and give yourself a few quiet minutes. No multitasking. No doomscrolling. Just a small pause to let your thoughts settle.

You're doing important work. And you don't have to sprint through it.

You can move forward one clear step at a time.

—Mary

SUPER PEP TALK #10

Hey friend—

If you're feeling a little buzzy after that chapter… totally normal.

Succession planning is a high-stakes decision, and it's often very visible in the organization. It touches risk, pressure, office politics, and people's futures. Even when you're doing it thoughtfully, your nervous system can still be like, *"Cool cool cool… but also AHHH."*

So before you jump into your next task, let's get you centered.

I want you to do a short guided visualization with me called **"How to Protect Your Peace."** It's designed to help you slow down, breathe deeper, and come back to yourself so you can move forward calm, clear, and steady.

Put your phone on Do Not Disturb.

Find a comfortable seat.

Unclench your jaw. Drop your shoulders.

And let your brain exhale for a minute.

Scan this QR code to listen to:

How to Protect Your Peace
(guided visualization)

You don't have to carry the weight of "getting it all right" at once.

You're doing meaningful work.

And you're allowed to protect your peace while you do it.

—Mary

SUPER PEP TALK #11

Hey friend—

Time for a quick re-centering moment.

You're probably buzzing with a bunch of new ideas after that chapter, huh?

Before you jump into your next task, let's help your body catch up to your brain.

Here's your quick reset:

- Put both feet on the floor.
- Inhale through your nose for 4.
- Hold for 2.
- Exhale slowly for 6.
- Repeat three times.

Now, if you want a guided version (with me in your ear), let's go!

Scan this QR code to listen to:

How to Calm Your Nerves
(guided visualization)

Give yourself this moment. You're allowed to slow down.

You're doing meaningful work. And you don't have to do it in a stressed-out state.

—Mary

SUPER PEP TALK #12

Hey friend—

Need a spark of creativity? Let's do something delightfully simple.

Right here on this page, grab a pen and draw one long squiggly line.

No planning. No stopping. No lifting your pen off the paper. Just let it wander while you doodle for a minute or two.

Now… look at your squiggle the way you'd look at clouds and start turning it into something. Add a few details. A couple circles. Some shading. See what shapes show up. Maybe it becomes a lightning bolt, a wave, a flower, a face, a new logo idea, or something totally random and abstract.

It does not have to look "good."

This isn't art class. This is you unlocking your right-brain creativity for 60 seconds.

Let it be messy. Let it be funny. Definitely let it look like a kid drew it.

The goal isn't perfection. The goal is motion.

And you might be surprised what shows up when you give yourself permission to play.

—Mary

SUPER PEP TALK #13

Hey friend—

Pause for a second. Take a breath.

You just finished the New Hire Onboarding chapter, and I want you to zoom out and notice something: you've learned a lot. And more importantly, you've been putting this playbook into action.

Have you had a few stumbles along the way? Of course. That's normal. That's how real change works.

Now ask yourself:

- What feels easier than it did a few chapters ago?
- What do you feel more confident doing now... simply because you've done it?

That's progress. That's you building momentum.

And here's the big picture: every small improvement you make in onboarding helps someone feel less lost, more welcomed, and more set up to succeed. Even if it only makes one person's work experience better, that's a WIN.

Keep going. You're doing meaningful work!

—Mary

SUPER PEP TALK #14

Hey friend—

Quick Reset Before You Lose Your Ish

HR Bingo (because… of course)

Check off what happened this week:

__ Someone said, "Quick question…" *(it was not quick)*

__ A "15-minute sync" became a 45-minute therapy session

__ You got asked to "just whip up" a policy… by EOD

__ Someone didn't read the email, then asked what the email said

__ A leader asked for "engagement ideas" but not "a lot of change"

__ You played calendar Tetris like it's an Olympic sport

__ A new hire didn't have access to the system they need… *again*

__ You said "happy to help!" while silently screaming

__ Someone replied-all to 38 people for no reason

__ You fixed something no one will notice *(except you)*

__ Someone was talking on a video call… but they were on mute. *(GROAN.)*

__ A "fire drill" hit and you had to drop everything and reshuffle your whole day for something (relatively) unnecessary

__ That curmudgeon didn't say good morning… *again.* Even though you've been trying to soften them up for months now

If you checked even **one** of these, congratulations: *you are doing heroic work.*

Now take one breath. Roll your shoulders back. Drink some water.

Then pick **one** next step and keep it moving.

You're not alone. We've all been there. Welcome to the club.

—Mary

SUPER PEP TALK #15

Hey friend—

If that chapter made your brain feel like it has 47 tabs open, you're not alone. Digital employee experience can get *real* technical, real fast.

So let's close a few tabs and get some headspace.

Here's your reset: **take your shoes off and put your feet in the grass.**

Yes, really.

Stand there for one minute. Feel the ground. Breathe slow. Let your body settle.

Will your coworkers look at you funny? Maybe.

Who cares. You're regulating your nervous system like a pro.

Now come back in, pick **one** idea from the chapter you want to explore next, and move forward one step at a time.

—Mary

SUPER PEP TALK #16

Hey friend—

If that chapter left your brain a little overloaded, you're not alone. Digital employee experience can feel like a flood of tools, systems, and super techy jargon… and your nervous system is like, "Greaaaaaaaat, love this for us."

So before you move on, let's do a reset together.

I want you to listen to this guided visualization with me: **"How to Let It Go."**

It's a simple way to release the mental clutter, soften your shoulders, and come back to center so you can move forward calm and clear.

Put your phone on Do Not Disturb.

Find a comfy seat.

Unclench your jaw.

And let yourself exhale.

Scan this QR code to listen to:

How to Let it Go
(guided visualization)

You don't have to hold every detail in your head.

Simple beats complicated. Every time. Choose the simplest action that creates real progress.

—Mary

SUPER PEP TALK #17

Before you walk into that conversation with Facilities, take a breath.

You're not going in to demand a fancy redesign or ask for a huge budget. You're going in as a partner with a clear goal:

Make work easier. Make work better.

Facilities teams are usually juggling a million constraints: space, safety, cost, timelines, vendor drama… and, let's be real, a faulty A/C unit that's either an arctic tundra or a swampy sauna. So lead with curiosity, not a mile-long wish list.

Here's your simple opener:

"Hey, I'd love to partner with you. We're looking at workplace experience through the lens of performance and well-being. Can we walk the space together and identify 1–2 small changes we could test in the next 30 days?"

Then ask three easy questions:

- Where do you see the biggest friction points right now?
- What's one low-lift improvement we could try fast?
- What would success look like from your side?

Remember: you're not pitching "culture." You're solving real problems. Noise. Focus. Flow. Collaboration. Comfort. Safety.

Keep it practical. Keep it human. Keep it simple.

You've got this.

PS: Maybe bring snacks.

—Mary

SUPER ~~PEP TALK~~ BONUS PAGE(!) #18

Hey friend—bonus resource time.

If you just finished the Workplace Experience chapter and thought, "Okay… but what do we *do* on anchor days?" this is for you.

This is a 15-minute Anchor Day Template you can copy and use immediately. It's simple on purpose. It doesn't require a big budget, a giant committee, or a 24-slide rollout plan.

Just three short moments that make the office feel more intentional:

1. Help people land
2. Create connection
3. Close the loop

Pick a day. Try it once. Adjust as you go.

15-Minute Anchor Day Template

Goal: Make the office feel worth it in 15 minutes total, without blowing up anyone's calendar.

Copy this template and try it on your next anchor day.

When	Time	What Happens	Where	Owner	What "Good" Looks Like
Start of day	5 min	Warm Welcome + Today's Anchor (one sentence: "Here's what we're here to do together today.")	Team area or a huddle spot	Team lead	People feel oriented, not rushed
Midday	5 min	Connection Moment (stand-up style share: "What are you working on this week?" and "Where are you stuck?")	Café or an open space	Anyone	New cross-team connections, quick help unlocked
End of day	5 min	Close the Loop (share: "What was one win from today?" and "One friction to fix tomorrow.")	Same huddle spot	Team lead	Clear takeaways and one improvement idea logged

Try these prompts

- **Start of day:** "Today's anchor is: _______. If you need help, ask early."
- **Connection moment:** "What are you working on?" / "What do you need?"
- **End of day:** "Win of the day?" / "One friction we can fix next time?"

Keep it simple. Keep it human.

And if you only do one part of this template, do the last 5 minutes. Closing the loop is where trust gets built.

Time to #DoTheThing!

—Mary

SUPER PEP TALK #19

Hey friend—

That chapter had a lot of moving parts. So before you jump back into your day, let's get you centered and clear.

Here's a simple reset: **box breathing.**

(Think: calm body = clear mind.)

Repeat this 3 times:

1. Breathe in for **4**
2. Hold for **4**
3. Breathe out for **4**
4. Hold for **4**

As you do it, drop your shoulders. Unclench your jaw. Let your brain slow down.

Keep it simple. One calm breath, then one clear choice.

—Mary

SUPER PEP TALK #20

Hey friend—

If that chapter lit a little fire in you (the good kind), I've got a perfect follow-up.

Because being a better people leader isn't about having the "right" personality. It's about choosing a few steady behaviors that make people feel safe, seen, and supported… even when work is messy.

When you want a simple boost (and a few practical ideas), press play.

Scan this QR code to listen to:

How to Be a Joy-Centered People Leader

featuring Sheryl Raphael Whitaker

This one is a breath of fresh air. Practical. Human. And it'll remind you that joy isn't extra credit. It's leadership.

—Mary

SUPER ~~PEP TALK~~ BONUS PAGE(!) #21

Need help turning culture into a five-slide executive pitch?

Hey friend—this is where culture gets taken seriously. When your ELT want an update on how the EX work you're doing is going, now is your time to shine. Drive home this message:

Better EX = Better CX = Better Business Results

Lead with a clear recommendation (of what you want them to do next), then walk them through a five-slide update in five minutes or less:

Baseline → Action → Result → Next Bet → Ask

Slide One: Recommendation (Lead with this)

- One-sentence recommendation
- Why now (one sentence)
- Decision needed today (approve / pilot / expand)

Slide Two: Baseline (What's happening, present day)

- 2–3 data points (EX + CX + business)
- One short frontline story (real, specific)
- What it's costing (time, churn, quality, revenue, risk)

Slide Three: Action (What we changed with EX)

- What we did (in plain English)
- Who it impacted (scope)
- What improved in the employee experience

Slide Four: Result (Proof)

- 3–5 metrics max
- Drive home the impact: Better EX → Better CX → Better Business Results
- One sentence: Here's what we learned

Slide Five: Next Bet + Ask (Here's what's next)

- Next bet (test or scale)
- What it unlocks (impact)
- The ask (budget / headcount / tools / policy)
- Timeline and success measures

Use This AI Prompt

"Write a five-slide narrative for senior leaders: Lead with the recommendation first (as concise as possible, what I want them to do next), then go into the problem, why it matters, what we changed, results with numbers, next bet, and the budget ask. Tone: direct and professional. Help me identify one short and compelling frontline story from our organization that drives this narrative. Do not make anything up."

Executives don't need more context and they certainly don't need a long-winded presentation.

They need clarity: one recommendation, one story, a few numbers, one ask.

—Mary

SUPER ~~PEP TALK~~ BONUS PAGE(!) #22

1-Page Culture Scorecard Template (Copy + Use)

You don't need 25 metrics. You need 5–7 you can publish every quarter and track long enough for the trend lines to mean something.

Cadence: monthly pulse + quarterly reset. Stay consistent.

Culture Scorecard (keep it one page!)

Metric (Lead/Lag)	Definition	Owner	Cadence	If It Moves, We Will...
Employee Net Promoter Score - eNPS (Lag)	% Promoters – % Detractors on "Recommend as a place to work"	HR	Quarterly	Prioritize top driver(s) and launch 30-day fix
Manager Effectiveness (Lead)	Avg score on 3–5 manager questions (clarity, support, feedback)	HR + Leaders	Quarterly	Target enablement for lowest-scoring group
Regrettable Attrition (Lag)	% of regretted exits / total headcount	HRBP	Quarterly	Diagnose hotspots and retention actions
Internal Mobility (Lag)	% roles filled internally	Talent	Quarterly	Improve career paths and internal hiring process
Burnout Risk (Lead)	% reporting unsustainable workload/stress	HR	Monthly	Reduce top friction and rebalance workload
Customer Proxy (Lag)	Customer satisfaction score (CSAT) or Net Promoter Score (NPS) for the customer segment or teams in scope (if available)	CX/Ops	Quarterly	Connect EX change to CX outcomes and adjust the next bet
Productivity Proxy (Lag)	Cycle time, quality metric, or backlog trend for teams in scope (pick one primary metric)	Ops	Quarterly	Scale what's working or stop what isn't

Use This AI Prompt

"Create a one-page culture scorecard for a _____-person hybrid company. Include 5–7 metrics split into lead and lag. For each metric, include the definition, owner, cadence, and what decision we make if it moves. Map it as an editable table to serve as a scorecard."

Measure what matters, then make the next bet.

—Mary

ACKNOWLEDGMENTS

Through this journey, I've learned that writing a book is a lot like completing a triathlon. There are three distinct phases to the process:

- Writing (the swim)
- Editing (the bike)
- Marketing and Speaking (the run)

It goes without saying, it's a lot. Each phase requires its own set of skills, focus, and muscles you never knew you had. I still remember the first time I signed up for a triathlon. I was absolutely terrified.

Sure, I knew how to do all of those three things separately, *but never all in one go!*

But I did it anyway.

I trained. I practiced. I made mistakes along the way. And I learned a lot that prepared me for the next one.

This book has been an incredible journey, very similar to what it feels like to do another lap in the pool, go one more mile on the bike, or tackle another hill on the treadmill.

Just show up every day and do the thing.

This process has stretched me in immeasurable ways, and I certainly could not, nor would I want to, have done it alone.

Thank you to book coach Kelley Rose for guiding me through phase one, the developmental stage that kickstarted the book now in your hands. Her encouragement to "just start writing" gave me the spark I needed to get the ideas swirling in my head out onto the page.

I was seeing the challenges my HR colleagues were facing and the unreasonable expectations they were carrying, and I knew the timing was right, especially in such a fast-changing HR industry. That spark inspired me to build the entire EX Flywheel as the heart of this playbook. Kelley's second set of eyes helped me crystallize and simplify the words, the tools, and the vision.

Thank you to my technical team: Zoe Norvell for the interior book design, and Suzen Marie and Jeffrey Lynn, my longtime partners who help edit *The Simplifiers Podcast* and the audiobook version of this book. None of this would be possible without them.

A great big thank you to every HR superstar, author, and thought leader who contributed their genius to this book, including everyone who shared real-world case studies, and to my early readers who pored over these pages and helped me simplify my words in powerful ways.

Thank you to my past, present, and future Simplifiers, including you, my reader, for choosing a better way to live.

My inner circle, the people I lovingly call **#TeamMary,** is an incredible collective of brilliant, heart-centered humans who inspire me, including Marrilee, Rosita, Patty, Jack, Xaviera, Doryan, Audrey, Carlos, and Charles. They have been my running partners this past year, advising me, opening doors, asking hard questions, sending me love, and cheering me on every step of the way.

A special shoutout to Kim, Stephenie, Rudy, Doris, Shane, Kristen, Wendy, Kristin, Jennifer, Kaira, Mark, Nicci, Heather, Colin, Antony, Alycia, Aubri, and Sarah for keeping me sane.

I'm so lucky to have them all in my life, and I hope everyone gets to experience this kind of support. They make my life that much richer.

And finally, to my family: Zoë, Otto, Zig, Vicki, and my dad. Thank you for loving me and supporting me in your own unique ways. And thank you for not squashing my dreams when I come to you with wild, crazy ideas like writing a book.

Let's squash the Sunday Scaries instead and help millions of people who feel stuck in corporate life fall back in love with work.

NOTES

Introduction

05   **First came "quiet quitting":** Zaid Khan, "Exploring the Quiet Quitting Trend," TikTok, July 25, 2022, https://www.tiktok.com/@zaidleppelin/video/7124414185282391342 and Cal Newport, "The Year in Quiet Quitting," The New Yorker, December 29, 2022, https://www.newyorker.com/culture/2022-in-review/the-year-in-quiet-quitting.

05   **Then came "quiet cracking":** Holger Reisinger, "'Quiet Cracking': A Loud Wake-Up Call For Business Leaders," Forbes Business Development Council, March 06, 2026, https://www.forbes.com/councils/forbesbusinessdevelopmentcouncil/2026/03/06/quiet-cracking-a-loud-wake-up-call-for-business-leaders.

06   **And now, I call it "simply surviving,":** That's all me. I coined that phrase. Because in this day in age with all that's happening in and outside of work, it certainly feels like that, huh?

06   **Gallup's 2025 State of the Global Workplace report:** State of the Global Workplace 2025, Gallup, 2025, https://www.gallup.com/workplace/349484/state-of-the-global-workplace.aspx.

08   **burnout prevention, retention, and trust-building:** Society for Human Resource Management, "2025 SHRM State of the Workplace," SHRM, March 12, 2025, https://www.shrm.org/topics-tools/research/2025-shrm-state-of-the-workplace

08 **88% of HR professionals:** The HRCI Team, "Post-COVID, HR Professionals Are Looking to Play a Larger Role in Business Operations " HRCI, December 04, 2024, https://www.hrci.org/blogs-and-announcements/press-releases/2024/12/04/hrci-2024-hr-role-post-covid-survey

10 **just like your favorite choose-your-own-adventure books:** Nothing brings me greater joy than the fact that I was able to incorporate this idea into this book for you! I loved these books as a kid and it's just a lovely reminder that you, my friend, are the hero of this story and you get to decide how and where you head next to make a positive impact at work. You've got this, now do the thing, and turn the page!

Chapter One

21 **A five-phase closed-loop system:** When doing this, make sure to not skip a step. Following this method, in this exact order: Collect → Interpret → Action Plan → Do The Thing → Report Back. Repeat for every Employee Listening cycle you run, in order to close the loop with your employees.

Chapter Two

56 **bad Glassdoor reviews pile up:** Have you checked your company's Glassdoor reviews lately? Visit www.glassdoor.com and search for your organization to see what former employees are saying. These reviews often come from people who felt strongly enough about their experience to take the extra step to write about it publicly. Yes, they may represent the more frustrated end of the spectrum, but if you're seeing the same themes come up again and again, it's worth paying attention. Repeated patterns are often a signal that there's an area of the employee experience worth auditing and improving.

Chapter Three

87   **Real-World Case Study:** A., Li, D. Benson and K. Shue, "Promotions and the peter principle," The Quarterly Journal of Economics, 2019, 2085-2134.

87   **Real-World Case Study:** F.L. Schmidt and J.E. Hunter, "The validity and utility of selection methods in personnel psychology: Practical and theoretical implications of 85 years of research findings," Psychological bulletin, 1998, 124(2), 262.

87   **Real-World Case Study:** J.E. Schleu and J. Hüffmeier, "Simply the best? A systematic literature review on the predictive validity of employee performance for leader performance," Human Resource Management Review, 2021, 31(2), 100777.

Chapter Four

106   **Match mentors and mentees based on the next skill or capability to build:** And don't forget the fact that powerful mentoring relationships are a two-way street. That's called "reverse mentoring," where the mentee could teach the mentor a few things as well. When pairing people together, consider what both parties could offer by way of skillbuilding to one another.

Chapter Five

124   **Twice a year, simulate a sudden vacancy:** I love this exercise, not because I want you or your teams imagining worst-case scenarios, but because life happens. People may need a leave of absence to care for an aging parent or family member. Or they may get recruited away by another company offering better pay, more flexibility, or the title they've been working toward. Whatever the reason, be prepared. Get your people thinking about what happens to the business if someone exits stage left and you need to recover fast.

Chapter Six

139   **The 6 A's of Event Design:** Julia Rutherford Silvers, CSEP, "The 6 A's of Event Design,"Professional Event Coordination (The Wiley Event Management Series), Second Edition, January 24, 2012.

Chapter Seven

161   **there are four questions every new hire wants answered before day one:** Alayna Click-Thomas, MS, SHRM-SCP, Magnet Culture, 2025, https://www.linkedin.com/in/alayna-thomas.

Chapter Eight

177   **Ownership is shared:** A word of warning: some of these stakeholders may push back on HR sniffing around their work. You may hear, "Stay in your lane. We've got this." That's okay. HR still has a responsibility to help ensure the digital employee experience is just as effective as the in-real-life employee experience. Tread lightly, build strong working relationships over time, and remember: you'll catch more flies with honey.

Chapter Nine

195   **Non-negotiables for a modern office space:** These are my non-negotiables, but your employees may have a different list. Bottom line: do not assume. Always ask them what they need in a modern workspace to do their jobs effectively.

214   **only 27% of managers are engaged at work globally:** State of the Global Workplace 2025, Gallup, 2025, https://www.gallup.com/workplace/349484/state-of-the-global-workplace.aspx.

Chapter Ten

218 **terrible bosses make for terrible jobs:** Young Entrepreneur Council (YEC), "12 Traits Bad Bosses Have in Common" Forbes, September 25, 2018, updated April 14, 2022, https://www.forbes.com/councils/theyec/2018/09/25/12-traits-bad-bosses-have-in-common.

Chapter Eleven

245 **Truth is, culture is everyone's job:** And yet, somehow, it still lands on your desk. If you want your executive leadership team to take ownership, you have to show them the numbers. How is this saving the company money or making the company money? When you can tell that story clearly, you earn buy-in at the top. Then you have to train your people leaders and managers, over and over again, to understand that they are culture champions who set the tone across the organization. They are the front line of culture change, both positive and negative.

Conclusion

261 **The Flywheel runs in two speeds: monthly and quarterly:** Monthly cycles are for quick wins. Quarterly cycles are for bigger employee experience initiatives. Some levers can be pulled at the same time and run in parallel, while others need to happen in sequence.

262 **Karen from Finance:** Fun fact, *Karen from Finance* is also the name of a brilliantly talented Australian drag queen. Her work is impeccable. https://www.karenfromfinance.com.

Super Pep Talk Pages

299 **box breathing:** The concept was originally coined by U.S. Navy SEAL, Mark Divine in 2006 to help special operations candidates

maintain calm and focus under extreme stress. It is based on ancient yoga *pranayama* techniques (specifically *sama vritti*) involving equal inhalations, holds, and exhalations. https://www.psychologytoday.com/us/blog/click-here-for-happiness/202309/how-to-use-box-breathing-for-well-being.

Bonus Note

One of the hardest parts of writing, editing, and publishing a book is realizing that not every great idea can stay on the page.

Originally, I included a carefully curated collection of quotes from popular TV shows, movies, and work-themed songs at the start of each chapter. They were funny, sharp, and painfully relatable. My hope was to give you a little chuckle at the absurdity of some of the worst parts of corporate life. Because honestly, if we cannot laugh at some of this, *what are we even doing?*

From Dolly Parton to The Office, Succession, The IT Crowd, Elf, Office Space, The Devil Wears Prada, Severance, and more, these cultural references captured so much of what feels broken at work today.

In the final stages of publishing, I had to remove them from the book. Painful, I know.

So, as a compromise, I created a curated playlist and companion page with the songs and clips that inspired those chapter openers. You can find them on the Bonus Resources page here: www.thesimplifiers.com/squash-book-bonus

It is not quite the same, but I am grateful for the artists, writers, and creators whose work made me laugh, think, and feel a little less alone on the hardest workdays.

Think of it as a small Easter egg waiting for you there.

ABOUT THE AUTHOR

Mary Baird, PHR, is a Senior Employee Experience Strategist, keynote speaker, and workshop facilitator who has spent more than 18 years helping organizations transform how people experience work. As the Founder of The Simplifiers, she partners with Fortune 500 companies, global enterprises, and high-growth startups to help leaders listen better, fix what's broken, and build workplaces where people fall back in love with work.

Mary has led training strategy architecture for Samsung Electronics America, advised executives on employee engagement and change management, and developed leadership programs that have measurably improved performance and retention. Earlier in her career, she produced award-winning, large-scale employee engagement events for clients like Google, Microsoft, Meta, Intel, and Electronic Arts, seeing firsthand how shared experiences shape culture and connection.

She is also the host of The Simplifiers Podcast, a globally recognized show with listeners in more than 155 countries and over 400 interviews featuring executives, authors, and thought leaders on leadership, culture, and the future of work. Her work has been featured in *Forbes, Newsweek, The Huffington Post, MSN, The Times,* and *Metro,* and she was named one of *Special Events* magazine's Top 25 Young Event Pros to Watch.

Mary's superpower is making the complex simple, helping leaders apply what they learn in practical ways to rebuild trust, empower people, and create workplaces that actually work. Through her speaking, consulting, and writing, she is on a mission to help HR and people leaders design employee experiences that rebuild trust, fuel performance, and build cultures where the Sunday Scaries don't stand a chance.

She lives in the Dallas–Fort Worth area, fosters pugs through DFW Pug Rescue, and loves bringing people together through community dinner parties. A former triathlete and avid traveler, she's on a mission to scuba dive in every major ocean—and to make Mondays something people actually look forward to again.

To learn more about the work she does in the world, visit:

www.marybaird.co

and

www.thesimplifiers.com